SPROUSE'S
TWO-EARNER
MONEY BOOK

Also by Mary L. Sprouse

How to Survive a Tax Audit

Taxable You:
Every Woman's Guide to Taxes

Sprouse's Income Tax Handbook

MARY · L. · SPROUSE

SPROUSE'S
TWO-EARNER
MONEY
BOOK

MAKING YOUR MONEY WORK
AS HARD AS YOU DO

VIKING

VIKING
Published by the Penguin Group
Viking Penguin, a division of Penguin Books USA Inc.,
375 Hudson Street, New York, New York 10014, U.S.A.
Penguin Books Ltd, 27 Wrights Lane, London W8 5TZ, England
Penguin Books Australia Ltd, Ringwood, Victoria, Australia
Penguin Books Canada Ltd, 2801 John Street,
Markham, Ontario, Canada L3R 1B4
Penguin Books (N.Z.) Ltd, 182-190 Wairau Road,
Auckland 10, New Zealand

Penguin Books Ltd, Registered Offices:
Harmondsworth, Middlesex, England

First published in 1991 by Viking Penguin,
a division of Penguin Books USA Inc.

1 3 5 7 9 10 8 6 4 2

PUBLISHER'S NOTE
This publication is designed to provide accurate and authoritative information in regard to the subject matter covered. It is sold with the understanding that the publisher is not engaged in rendering legal, accounting or other
professional service. If legal advice or other expert assistance is required,
the service of a competent professional person should be sought.

LIBRARY OF CONGRESS CATALOGING IN PUBLICATION DATA
Sprouse, Mary L.
Sprouse's two-earner money book : making your money work as hard
as you do / Mary L. Sprouse.
p. cm.
Includes index.
ISBN 0-670-83115-8
1. Dual-career families—Finance, Personal. 2. Finance, Personal.
I. Title. II. Title: Two-earner money book.
HG179.S558   1991
332.024—dc20   91-50144

Printed in the United States of America
Set in Times Roman
Designed by Victoria Hartman

CONTENTS

v

SPROUSE'S
TWO-EARNER
MONEY BOOK

1

INTRODUCTION:
Double Your Treasure, Double Your Funds

Want a quick course in the psychology of investing? Watch "Wheel of Fortune." At the end of the show, the day's Big Winner has to make a choice. An investment decision, really.

"Charlie," host Pat Sajak says, "tell us what she can win."

"Certainly, Pat. Donna, you can pick this magnificent hand-woven Persian carpet worth $84,000. Or," and here there is a drum roll, "solve the puzzle and win good old American cash totaling $25,000."

Seems like an obvious choice, doesn't it? But no one ever goes for the carpet, even though it's worth more than three times the cash.

Granted, a carpet has drawbacks. You have to report it as income, but you can't whack off a third of it to pay the tax. And, if you want to sell, you probably need a Turkish uncle to get every dollar's worth.

But I think the reason every contestant chooses cash is that we all recognize the value of a dollar. Put most of us in a room with an $84,000 carpet on which someone has dropped a quarter, and we'll pocket the quarter, feeling

1

pretty pleased with ourselves. True value often goes unrecognized.

The value of marriage, for instance. You be the contestant this time. Your choice of prizes: a law degree, a $200,000 inheritance, or marriage to a spouse who works.

If you're reading this book because you're half of a two-earner couple, you already made the right choice. Probably without meaning to, you took the smartest financial step of your life when you took your spouse's paycheck in marriage.

We're not used to thinking of marriage in economic terms any more than we do carpets. So you may not know that marriage—in addition to its other virtues—is the modern key to wealth. In fact, a study by the University of Michigan Institute for Social Research concluded that being married is more important to your financial well-being today than your education, skills, or attitude toward work.

Let's back that up with numbers. According to a Census Bureau survey released in 1985, households headed by married couples had a median net worth of $50,116, compared with $13,885 for households headed by unmarried females and $9,883 for those headed by unmarried men. How's that for extra icing on the wedding cake?

Couples who work have a tremendous edge in achieving today's version of the good life. Not because two can live more cheaply than one, but because they can *earn* more than one.

In Las Vegas casinos, the big draw is a chance to Double Your Paycheck. The appeal is evident. If you win, you can pay your bills with your regular wages. The second paycheck is discretionary income. You can use it to paint the town red or, if you're wise, to save and invest.

Two-earners earn a double paycheck every payday. And that is an enormous advantage in accumulating wealth, because excess earnings after buying necessities can grow dramatically over time.

Fixed payments for essentials, such as food, shelter, and transportation, consume more than 40% of a family's income. For George, who earns $30,000 annually and is the sole breadwinner, that leaves $18,000 discretionary income (60% of his $30,000 income). If he invests the entire $18,000 at 8%, compounded monthly, George can retire in 20 years with $88,682.

Ron and Linda earn twice as much and, therefore, have twice as much discretionary income. Their $36,000 invested at the same rate of interest will grow to $177,364.

So what are you doing with all that wealth? Weekending in Monte Carlo, riding to the hounds, stretching your limo? After all, you earn—and spend—more in one year than earlier generations even fantasized about. As recently as 1947, the median family income was well under $6,000 in current dollar values. Today, joint incomes between $60,000 and $120,000 are commonplace.

"We don't understand," more than a few of my two-earner clients wail. "We make more money than we ever dreamed possible. Why do we feel so poor?"

You know the stereotype—modern couples craving instant gratification, BMWs, and room-sized entertainment centers. They would spend even more if they had the time. The yuppie life is only a Madison Avenue dream for many couples, though. Despite lofty earnings, most of us are taking a licking on a number of economic fronts: competition for higher-paying jobs by crowds of baby boom applicants, slower economic growth, higher real interest rates, higher social security taxes, and costly time-saving services.

Meanwhile, your income is losing the race with inflation. Although median family income rose 150.6% between 1972 and 1987, inflation climbed 168.4%. Housing prices broke all existing records—the cost of a new house shot up 294%. Existing home prices rose 222%.

If you don't already own a home, saving for a down payment is difficult because of higher rents—a result of tax reform. In fact, two incomes are usually needed to buy a house, and even then, most first-time home buyers have only three-fourths of the income required to carry a mortgage at today's rates.

The result has been a dramatic decline in your ability to pursue the American dream: a home, your children's education, and financial security. Economists say that, financially, couples are worse off than their counterparts at the same age ten to twenty years ago.

And what about the future? The good news is that you're likely to live as long as 20 years after you retire. The problem—besides blowing out the candles—is building up enough savings to keep buying birthday cakes. Social security will barely pay for the party hats. Your benefits will amount to only $13,000 a year in current dollars if you retire after 2012.

It gets worse. Listen to what Americans for Generational Equity, a special-interest group, has to say: "The baby boom generation . . . will collectively face a disastrous retirement and . . . its children will . . . be much more heavily burdened with the support of its parents than any other generation in history."

Worried? Good. Angry? Even better. You have to know what you're up against before you charge into battle. Ask Custer. You have a tough fight on your hands, but you already have two big guns in your favor—those two paychecks. Singles and families with one earner are a lot more likely to get scalped.

Of course, packing the most guns won't help unless you

know how to shoot straight. Wall Street abounds with tales of investors who parlayed a few dollars into vast fortunes, while lottery millionaires blundered back into poverty.

Chances are that you knew what you wanted to be when you grew up, and chances are that it had nothing to do with managing money. You knew you wanted money—preferably lots of it—but that would be a happy by-product of your creative, exciting, high-powered career.

Take my clients, Glen and Susan. Soft-spoken, with the reserve of a man more comfortable with differential equations than people, Glen is a highway engineer. Susan, outgoing, is a cardiac care nurse. Together, they earn close to $110,000 a year. What do they have to show for it? Nothing. With what, until recently, would have been considered a small fortune, Glen and Susan own no home, no income-producing real estate, no stocks or mutual funds. They have less than $3,000 in a savings account, no tax write-offs other than state income taxes, and no plans for retirement or sending their two children to college.

Between them, Glen and Susan have 11 years of higher education, but not one course in finance. In 10 years, more than a million dollars will slip through their fingers. All because neither knows any more about managing income than their parents who earned $10,000 a year.

"We're wage earners," Glen says. Wage earners, his tone implies, don't expect to get rich. If there's anything left over on Saturday night, they sock it away in a passbook savings account and go bowling. They buy a modest house so the kids will have a yard to play in, not as the first step in some fool wealth-building scheme. How much finance do wage earners need to know?

They're an intelligent couple, but they don't take their earning power seriously. If the two of you are bringing home $110,000 (or even $50,000), you are more than mere wage earners. Like it or not, whatever your chosen professions, you are also in the business of money.

How can you work a 56-hour week, raise a family, and run a money business, too? How can you make the most of two incomes when making two incomes takes most of your time?

This book tells how to make your money work as hard as you do—without having to work hard to do it. You'll learn where to invest for the highest yields with the least time involvement. You'll find out how to choose the professional help you need and how to turn your computer into a personal money manager. And for those of you who want to get off to a quick start, there are investments you can run with tomorrow.

This is more than a general investment guide, however. It is also concerned with the financial and legal issues of particular interest to two-earner families, including money attitudes and how they affect a couple's investment strategies, how to hold title to joint property, homeownership, tax law for couples, managing a child's finances, providing for a child's college education, and estate planning.

Some of the material in the early chapters is elementary. If you analyze market averages for amusement, don't worry. The advice quickly becomes more sophisticated. Some of the material in the later chapters is highly technical. If you don't know a money market from a margin account, don't worry, either. You have to learn sometime, and explanations are in clear, uncluttered English. Whether you are financial innocents or battle-scarred veterans of investments wars, whether your finances have the spit and polish of an accounting brigade or are as messy as an unmade bed, you'll find invaluable information here on how to harness the power of your two incomes.

$ $ $

As a two-earner couple, you have forged a partnership that can conquer financial worlds. You are able to raise capital twice as quickly, capitalize on double the borrowing power, even gamble boldly on a business of your own, secure in your partner's income. The only limit is your commitment and drive.

This is a book to be shared. Whatever your financial goals, by working together with trust and love, you are twice as likely to reach them.

2

RECONCILABLE DIFFERENCES: Love and Money

What is Money to you? A defender, pretender, a despot, or savior? A sorcerer, a swindler, a seductress, a sinner?

Money is not a living, breathing thing, but most of us invest it with a personality. It's more than the dull, bloodless medium of commerce. We take it personally. We don't simply earn it, spend it, save it. We bless it, curse it, flash it, stash it, bet it, sweat it, lie for it, die for it.

The character we attribute to money springs from our past. Take down the family album. Turn to your childhood pictures. Your money attitudes were developed about the same time as the photos. Maybe you can't see the investors you've become in the freckled faces of yesterday. But there are memories, colored by money or the lack of it: a sea of presents or an empty stocking beneath the Christmas tree, cashmere sweaters or hand-me-downs, a shiny new bike or a busted wagon.

Your money values, hopes, fears, and wisdom were strongly shaped by your parents. The Depression, for example, had a profound inhibiting effect not only on the generation growing up in the thirties, but on their children as well. If you are in this group, as I am, you probably believe in savings bonds, distrust real estate, overrate job security, and will never feel you've saved enough. Just like your parents.

If you're lucky, you inherited mental wealth—money attitudes that ensure financial success. Your investment decisions are bold and flawless, you strike the perfect balance between enterprise and thrift, and you treat money as dispassionately as the Federal Reserve does.

If you're like most of us, however, you have financial phobias and hang-ups that block your path to fortune. Maybe it's a fear of loss that restricts you to sure things. Maybe it's a belief in luck that handicaps you into basing investments on little more than *The Racing Form*. Maybe you're a sucker for hot tips or you have cold feet. Maybe you expect money to buy power, happiness, or love. Whatever your quirks or foibles, they can lead to missed opportunities, irrational decisions, miserliness, or wanton spending.

Don't worry. You don't need therapy. Your money hang-ups are simply stumbling blocks. They can slow you down, not stop you. Base your investment decisions on facts, not feelings. Learn from your past mistakes without being traumatized by them.

Your own money attitudes may not warrant a psychoanalyst, but marry and you become a split money personality. Marriage is a melting pot of diverse money attitudes, expectations, and experiences. Monica expects to be surrounded by the luxuries she was denied as a girl, but Mark dreads the impoverished retirement his parents suffered. Ted is an armchair swashbuckler, taking risks as an escape from his humdrum job, while her father's bankruptcy left Karen wary of speculation.

Your financial success depends on how well you reconcile

your differences. The first step is discovering each other's values and attitudes about money. Don't expect miracles. No two people—no matter how much in love—are going to agree completely about anything, let alone money. In fact, there's no saying that skinflint Jerry can't find financial happiness with pound-foolish Eva. They have to work harder at it, that's all.

In toting up your differences, don't overlook the most basic difference of all: whether because of upbringing, social pressures, or experience, men and women view money in subtly different ways.

Take the very concept of wealth, for example. In answer to the question, "How much money makes you feel well off?" the men surveyed were likely to say $1,000,000. Women typically answered in the range of $30,000. Unless you define what you mean by success, therefore, you may think you're headed for the same goal only to find yourselves leagues apart.

What other money attitudes and spending habits distinguish men from women? According to a survey conducted for *Money* magazine, women are more likely to worry about money than men are. They are also more generous—40% said they would give part of a windfall to relatives or charity, compared to only 26% of the men. Men were more likely to invest the windfall, while women would spend it.

On the spending side, fewer women have credit cards than men and their credit purchases are smaller. Women on the average carry less cash than men.

Another *Money* poll shows that women trust more to luck than to their own efforts to achieve wealth. Yet women win handily at budgeting and bookkeeping.

In my own practice, I've observed that men's financial goals center around business, women's around home and family. Most men would like to be Donald Trump or Steven

Jobs. Few women have such entrepreneurial visions, perhaps because of the scarcity of role models. Women seem content to carve a niche in the business world; men pursue empires.

Men are more likely to devise elaborate moneymaking schemes. Some of these are as impractical and bizarre as early flying machines, but men at least jump off buildings with them, whereas women rarely try.

Women are painstaking researchers, substituting information gathering for making the first move. But this caution makes women less irresponsible about money. Men use money to generate excitement or wield power; women value money for security.

Women expect a dollar to buy more than men do. Women underestimate the value of professional services and are less willing to pay for expertise. This is true even of professional women who charge for their services. Men are much less price-conscious, saying, "Send me the bill," without asking the cost.

Both men and women still tend to view finance as a "man's job" and "unladylike." Women are willing accomplices, equating balancing a checkbook with changing spark plugs and price-earnings ratios with quantum physics. The harm is obvious. Lack of knowledge means lack of choices, and women invest in a much narrower range of investment vehicles than men do.

MONEY TALKS

Understanding each other's money attitudes will go a long way toward making you a winning team. You won't get your signals crossed. One of you won't go racing for the end zone, while the other throws for short yardage. You'll know that your spouse likes to run on third and long. Your spouse will know you like to pass.

Some disagreement is inevitable. From time to time, one of you will pull the ball away just as the other kicks. The culprit is almost always lack of communication. Don't get into a shouting match on the field. Get back in the huddle, and have a frank discussion.

Talking candidly about money contributes to your family's emotional, as well as financial, well-being. Putting a lid on discussion keeps you from bridging your differences, correcting inaccurate information that one of you has about your current financial situation, and losing sight of important goals.

But before you begin Round One, there are a few ground rules. Agree on what you're fighting over—the real reason, not the electric bagel cutter that set it off. Ask yourself what money attitude has been outraged or threatened, and direct the discussion to that.

Don't use money problems to vent anger that you feel about something else. Don't use money as a weapon, either, waging buying wars or withholding income as forms of retaliation. Money has the power to express love and protection, but it can be an equally powerful means of expressing hostility.

Keep the lines of communication open. If one of you runs into money difficulties, don't try to "protect" the other by keeping it a secret. He or she will still be following the agreed-upon financial plan, when all the rules have changed. Your spouse will be like a driver who leaves a passenger standing at the curb, thinking he's in the backseat.

Financial goals must be flexible to deal with new situations—the arrival of a baby, the purchase of a house, a promotion. Free and open channels of communication let you make rapid substitutions or change plays to meet changed conditions. That way your team always has the right resources in position to score.

Don't shut your children out. Silence deprives them of a valuable learning experience. If family finances are kept the parents' secret, your children may never learn how to handle money on their own.

Out of the process of sharing differences and resolving money disputes will emerge a matchless money style of your own. Let your tastes, talents, and enthusiasms inspire it. And be sure to add a generous measure of self-esteem. The most successful money masters possess unbounded confidence and feelings of personal worth.

CHECK MATES

"I've always been interested in accounting," one of my clients confided. "Right now, I'm in the plumbing end of it."

Right now, we're discussing the household end of it. Along with fixing the toaster, cleaning the shower, and ordering take-out, running a household means managing the money. This includes all the dull, mindless chores, like balancing the checkbook, as well as such debt-defying acts as investing and planning.

Before you can set your financial plans in motion, the two of you must work out an efficient and equitable method of money management. Unless you are newlyweds, you have probably already grappled with most of the burning issues. How should you split your incomes—if at all? Should you have joint or separate checking accounts? Whose income is spent for what items? When should you consult about major purchases and investment decisions? Who has the final say?

Who pays the bills, does the bookkeeping, prepares the tax return?

There are as many answers as there are couples. The details are not important, so long as neither of you feels cheated or used. Money management seems to run smoothest, however, when both spouses share responsibility and have an equal say over decisions.

As wage earners, you should both be financially adept. By that, I don't mean able to define dollar-cost averaging or debentures at the drop of a hat. But you should—indeed, must—know the basics of household finance as well as you know the difference between a flathead and a Phillips screwdriver or between a skillet and a crepe pan. If you don't, find time for togetherness, and let your spouse teach you.

Divvy up mastering the intricacies of high finance with my blessing. But *both* of you must learn the fundamentals of tax law. Protest all you want. It's not optional. One of your shared duties is record keeping, and the driving force behind record keeping is taxes. How can you do a competent job if you don't know which documents are tax-related? The same is true for preparing your tax returns. Whether you tackle the 1040 yourself or pass it along to a preparer, you both must know which information to gather. That's the mundane reason. There is a much headier one. Taxes are part of the big picture. You cannot intelligently spend, invest, or plan without tax knowledge.

Share the weighty, interesting tasks as well as the boring, tedious ones. One spouse shouldn't end up with a mop and all the bills, while the other looks all-knowing and studies the *Wall Street Journal.* Don't let the fact that one of you is (temporarily) earning more than the other tip the balance of power, either. This is a marriage, not global politics.

Women, especially, use ignorance as an excuse for shirking what should be a joint responsibility. Too many husbands are happy to oblige. After all, money is a traditional male stronghold. But succumbing to these stereotyped roles can have adverse consequences in the event of divorce or the death or incapacity of the husband. Both of you should be equally capable of shouldering responsibility for all family financial matters.

At the very least, both of you should know the source and amount of your spouse's income, the amount of life insurance each carries, whether your spouse is covered by a company pension plan, and the location of legal and financial documents.

For those of you just starting out or receptive to a little fine-tuning, here are some suggestions for banking, spending, managing, and investing your two incomes. In broad terms, they recommend that you (1) pool funds; (2) delegate authority; (3) share decisions; (4) operate like a business; and (5) use timesaving methods. If you already have a workable and mutually satisfying system for managing your finances, feel free to skip these basics.

1. Bank jointly. The way that money is managed and accounts are kept sends a subtle message. Pooled funds or jointly owned assets testify to your belief that marriage is a joint venture financially, professionally, and emotionally.

Sentiment aside, a single joint bank account means cutting down on paperwork and administrative fees. The fewer accounts of any kind, the better. Naturally, each of you should be authorized to sign checks.

To save check charges, enter only the amount in excess of the minimum required balance in your check register. For example, Tom and Peggy start a joint bank account by depositing $3,000. The bank exacts a service charge if the balance falls below $1,000, so Tom and Peggy enter only $2,000 ($3,000 deposit minus $1,000 minimum balance) in their check register.

You want to commit as little of your money as possible to the joint bank account. Why? Because a checking account is a loser. You should open one that pays interest, but at best, your earnings will be laughable. Use a money market account instead to pay large bills. Decide on the minimum you need to meet day-to-day living expenses, and *automatically* transfer excess funds to the money market account. There it will earn a respectable rate of return, while you decide at leisure where else to invest it.

Find a money market fund that permits unlimited check writing. Checks must generally be for at least $250 or $500. Use this account for all bills or purchases over this minimum amount.

If both of you aren't conscientious about recording checks and deposits, managing your joint account will be like trying to get rid of a feather with molasses on your fingers. I can't help you here. You have to discipline yourselves. This is the kindergarten of finance. If you can't keep your checkbook straight and finger-paint, what will you do when it comes time for college-level investing?

Once a month, one or the other of you will bring the two checkbooks together and make sure the account balances. See the discussion on delegating duties below.

Just as you may occasionally want time to yourself, you may want to have some money of your own. You don't have identical interests. One of you might want to save for a graduate degree, the other to build a sailboat. Or you may want to treat yourselves or buy each other gifts without having to reveal the cost.

In that case, pool the bulk of your incomes, and put the rest in separate accounts. Now decide how to split your incomes. You can make equal contributions to the common fund or contribute in proportion to your separate incomes. Costs must also be allocated. Which expenses will you treat as joint (food, shelter, vacations) and which as personal (clothing, gifts, child support, premarital debt)?

Do not use separate accounts to pay for tax-deductible expenses unless you intend to file separate tax returns. Otherwise, you will have too many trails to follow at tax time. See Chapter 7 for a discussion of the benefits of joint versus separate returns.

Each spouse should be responsible for the bookkeeping on his or her own individual account.

What are the advantages of separate accounts? You may be able to take advantage of free services that your bank offers new depositors. Separate accounts in different banks give you more places to turn for a loan in case of an emergency. And these accounts can provide needed funds if a joint account is closed because one spouse dies.

The drawbacks? More money tied up in required minimum balances, earning little or no interest. More fees. Less money committed to your shared financial plan.

2. Take credit together. You can ease your bookkeeping tasks and cut costs by carrying credit cards in your individual names on a joint account. Why waste time, checks, and postage by mailing two payments to the same company each month? Why double your annual membership fee? Besides, with two accounts it's harder to keep track of expenses, especially the tax-deductible ones.

Both of you need healthy credit histories. You should keep at least one or two credit cards in each of your own names to ensure that both of you will be able to obtain credit in case of divorce or death. Most bank cards, such as Mastercard and VISA, offer only individual accounts that permit "authorized secondary users," a status that carries little clout. The solution is for one spouse to be the "primary" cardholder on the Mastercard, for instance, and the other spouse to be the "primary" VISA cardholder.

To avoid exceeding your credit line, set a dollar limit on individual charges to joint accounts. Advance notice to the other spouse should be required before charging higher amounts.

You probably want separate credit cards for stores that only one of you frequents, such as clothing stores. Carry a separate business credit card if you travel or entertain for business and your employer doesn't provide one.

3. Delegate and rotate responsibility. Think of managing your money as running a small-town theater company—one where the producer is also in charge of lighting and props, while the director raises the curtain and paints the sets. Either one of them can do any job, from sweeping the aisles to standing in the limelight. Because, no matter what, the show must go on.

Both of you should be just as multifaceted and talented at money management. In the event of disability, death, overtime, or out-of-town meetings, your own show must go on. That means both of you must be able to act as stand-in.

Rotate money management duties so that you both gain experience in all aspects of finance. This also prevents one of you from getting stuck with boring chores or losing sight of the overall financial picture.

You can divide tasks equally, then switch jobs every six months. Or one of you can take charge completely for six months at a stretch. This latter arrangement may be the ticket if one of you is in a seasonal business or travels extensively at certain times of the year.

What if one of you invariably winds up balancing the checkbook or paying the bills because the other is constantly on the road? Consider a trade-off, where the wandering spouse assumes three or four big tasks, such as preparing the tax return or studying investment prospectuses (perfect hotel reading).

If one of you thinks you have superior ability in one area, you may be tempted to commandeer it. Why should you take turns doing bookkeeping when you are a C.P.A. and your spouse thinks double entry is a very big door? Well, for one thing, you probably weren't born with a general ledger in your hand. You spent years in classrooms entering debits and credits to become as proficient as you are. How is your spouse going to learn without doing? Take the time to teach your spouse elementary bookkeeping. Keeping the household books does not require full-scale accounting.

What if your ability is one that can't be taught—a magic touch? Every stock you've picked in the last three years has shot through the roof, for example. Terrific. Maybe your spouse should stand to one side to keep from being blinded by the light. But your track record should be *proven*. And remember that past success is no guarantee of equal success in the future. *Remember:* Math ability cannot be touted as financial talent. If it could, your pocket calculator would rank with Bernard Baruch.

Delegating authority is a great time-saver. You don't have to do everything in tandem. One of you can visit your tax preparer, meet with your banker, consult your insurance agent.

You should both be present the first time you meet with or engage an attorney, accountant, or stockbroker. Let professionals know that either of you has authority to make decisions and place orders. Thereafter, joint meetings can be limited to those times when the advice sought is of major import, when there is a possible conflict of interest between you and your spouse, or when two signatures are required.

4. Discuss financial goals and share decisions. Schedule periodic meetings to assess your financial status, confer about problems, and review your plans for the future. Use the time to make decisions about investments, major purchases, borrowing, and other money matters requiring joint agreement. Give these talks priority. Make an appointment if you have to. Treat it as a professional meeting, but a pleasurable one. Reserve a table at your favorite restaurant, bring your documents, and go over the scheduled topics as you would at any business dinner. (Unfortunately, the cost of a meal when only a husband and wife are present is not deductible, even though the purpose is to discuss business.)

5. Operate as a well-run business. You and IBM have the same goal—you want to make money. You stand your best chance to profit, therefore, if you operate like IBM. On a smaller scale, of course.

Go into the investment business. Transfer your combined knowledge of the business world to your family finances. Modify the reports, forms, controls, and filing systems you use at work to serve your needs at home. This initial time investment will pay dividends later.

Set aside a portion of your home as an office, furnish it, and lay in a stock of office supplies. Make sure there is work space for both of you at once.

Buy a filing cabinet for investment publications and articles and prospectuses. Use the same cabinet for your bookkeeping records. Each of you will file the receipts you bring home, and the cancelled checks written on your separate accounts. Filing the joint account checks will be a delegated duty. At regular intervals, summarize these records, preferably on computer.

Pay your children to help you. They can perform low-skill office jobs, such as filing, freeing you for more sophisticated activities. And if the wages are reasonable for the type of services rendered, they are deductible as an investment expense.

Your investment activity produces other tax deductions. You may write off the cost of office and computer supplies;

office furnishings (desks, chairs, filing cabinets); office equipment (typewriter, calculator); investment publications, books, and newsletters specifically related to investments you hold; and money management computer software (depreciated over five years).

You cannot claim an office-in-home deduction for managing investments. That means you cannot write off a portion of your rent or home cost, home insurance, repairs, or utilities. The IRS stands firm against deducting the cost of a computer for this purpose, too.

Investment expenses are deductible as miscellaneous itemized deductions on Schedule A, Form 1040, to the extent they exceed 2% of your adjusted gross income.

6. Form an investment club with your spouse. Nothing formal. You don't even need bylaws and a secret handshake. The purpose is to save time and let you both take part in choosing investments.

Decide what types of investments are needed to meet your specific goals, then assign them equally. For example, with secure jobs and 30 years to retirement, Steve and Pam decide they can afford an aggressive risk-taking strategy. They believe small-company growth stock offers the best chance for above-average returns over the long term. Because they are in the highest tax bracket, they also decide to round out their portfolio with tax-exempt bond funds. Steve might elect to research and select the stocks, while Pam does the same for bond funds. Or they might each agree to pick one stock and one fund.

Each of you would account for the performance of your chosen investments from time to time. You can even compete, for example, each picking a mutual fund and comparing results. Analyze why one outperformed the other and learn together.

Remember, even top money managers cannot consistently

pick winners. No blame should attach to the spouse whose investments are currently lagging behind.

TEST YOUR FINANCIAL COMPATIBILITY

Answer yes or no to the following questions and compare your responses. Discuss your differences. Make a list of areas of agreement, and use it as a guideline in making investments. Remember, there are no right or wrong answers.

1. If I had $100,000, I would still want to make more.
2. I feel guilty when I spend money that could be saved.
3. I would pick a promising growth stock over a blue-chip stock that had never missed a dividend.
4. I would rather live in a small house that is paid for than in a large house with a mortgage.
5. I would depend entirely on a broker or financial planner for all investment advice.
6. If the price of my stock started to fall, I would sell it immediately.
7. Quality is more important to me than price.
8. I would never loan money to a relative to start up a business.
9. I would rather pay more taxes than I have to than have problems with the IRS.
10. I never second-guess a spending or investment decision after I've made it.

3

OF TIME AND THE INVESTOR:
Making Your Money
Work As Hard As You Do

So much income, so little time. There you are, slaving to earn two paychecks that you scarcely have time to deposit, much less spend and invest. You see less sun than a groundhog, keep a change of clothes in the car, and couldn't pick Junior out of a lineup. Is it any wonder the hottest-selling item on the market today is time?

Juggling job, home, and family doesn't leave much time for finance. Is your money doomed to gather dust at 5¼%, while you stand knee-deep in bank statements and bills?

Of course not. You *can* work 30-hour days and manage your money, too. The same time management principles that work in the office serve just as well at home. If you let them, computers can make a few nanoseconds' work out of a month of checks, charge slips, and restaurant receipts. Or you can put your buying power to use by hiring a cadre of financial professionals.

Here's how to make time for your money:

SIMPLIFY YOUR FINANCIAL LIFE

Does it take three hours and a flamethrower to flush out a receipt? Then it's time to get organized. Every second spent rummaging could be better used deciphering a prospectus, charting stock prices, or, all right, renting *Ghostbusters*. You won't miss important due dates, either, and your records will be so precise, you'll never again pay more tax than you owe.

It's now or never, though. Until you hack through the jumble, you can't tackle the real business of money management—investing.

Clutter Busting

Buy a file cabinet. You have too many records to keep in a box under the bed. Besides, how often will you refer to them if you have to fight dust balls? Now buy dividers and use them. List all the categories of your records for the current year, and label the dividers. Keep prior-year tax records separate (see "Record Keeping" below).

Make a similar list of investment topics that you intend to collect information about, such as stocks, money market funds, home buying, and collectibles. Devote a divider to each of these subjects as well.

Now, in a burst of energy, file everything at once. If you're like most people, you'll never get around to it again. Then keep up with it. File, don't pile.

Next, spring for in- and out-baskets. Don't let them collapse under their own weight, however. That will only intimidate you. Pay bills when received and balance checkbooks monthly. Try to cluster due dates around the same time. For example, arrange for your house, car, and recreational vehicle payments to be payable on the first or fifteenth of every month. Invest in certificates of deposit that mature near the same date. Keep installment payments, and interest expense, to a minimum by paying off charges at once.

To alert you to matters requiring action, set up a home version of the "tickler" file lawyers use. You need 12 file folders, one for each month, with the current month in front. Behind the current month's file, add 31 day files. File documents or projects according to the day you must start work on them, not by the deadline. At the end of each month, transfer the now empty day files to the next month and start over.

Along similar lines, maintain separate financial calendars. Schedule "appointments" to attend to specific financial affairs. Don't forget to pencil in financial meetings with each other.

Consolidation

The first place to cut clutter is at the mailbox. Consolidate accounts and you can rent out your box.

Start by pitching unneeded plastic. You can probably get by with two major credit cards—one for personal purchases and one for business. If you need more purchasing power, ask for a higher credit limit. Besides having fewer bills to pay, you'll save on annual fees.

If you can't kick the credit habit that easily, at least discard cards on which you charge less than a fixed amount per year, say $500.

Combine bank accounts, too. As we've discussed, one joint checking account that pays interest is all you need. If you both want your own money, at least pay all household bills from one joint account.

Record Keeping

A well-oiled financial machine depends on good record keeping. This is especially true when both of you are performing financial duties. Your record-keeping system is where your activities meet and are coordinated. It is also a source of information about what the other is doing.

Good record keeping is not rocket science. All you need is determination and a dose of common sense. You don't have to know a debit from a credit. And you don't need ledgers and double-entry journals. Something less sophisticated will probably do, unless you own your own business or S corporation (a corporation that elects to be taxed like a partnership). In that case, find an accountant or bookkeeper to establish a set of books for the business.

Your file cabinet is the best place to store records. Simply tossing your records in, however, will *not* do. Instead, sort them into categories, and drop them behind labeled dividers.

You should have the following categories:

Income (wages, interest/ dividends, etc.)	Contributions
	Child care
Exemptions (cost of shelter, food, clothing, etc.)	Business expenses
	Automobile (one for each car)
Medical expenses	Travel
Taxes	Major purchases
Interest	Miscellaneous

If your finances are more diversified, you may want to add the following:

Home and home	Investments
improvements	Deeds
Rental property	Insurance
Escrow papers and	Legal and accounting
mortgages	

The above categories are the most universal and should cover most of your income and expenses. Everyone's life and work are unique, however. If yours includes anything from airplanes to zero-coupon bonds, feel free to improve upon the system.

Keep only the current year's records in the income and expense categories. When you have finished your taxes, file those records with the tax return in another part of your cabinet.

You want to keep every receipt, check, cash register tape, and charge slip for tax-deductible items. Don't make snap judgments on the run about deductibility. Stuff every scrap of paper in your pocket or purse, and sort them when you get home. Throw out the receipt for cat litter then. If a document fits into more than one category—for example, a home loan statement showing both interest and taxes—photocopy it or put a note behind one of the categories referring you to where it can be found.

There is no need to keep a daily journal. The one exception is for business mileage, where a log book is a must. Keep the log in your car and write down the mileage and the purpose of your trip each time you hit the road on business. If you entertain clients, I also recommend entering the restaurant name and cost in your appointment book.

Disposing of records. How long must your records take up valuable space? The general rule is that receipts may be discarded three years from the date the return is filed or due (or two years from the date the tax was paid, whichever is later).

Some records should be kept longer. If you own a business, save those records for seven years and employee records for four years. Receipts for major purchases should be saved for as long as you own the items.

Keep property records for as long as they are needed to determine the basis of the original property or the property that replaced it. For example, if you sell your first home and defer the gain by reinvesting in a more expensive property, save the escrow statements for the first home until you dispose of the second. If you again defer gain on the sale of the second home, retain escrow statements for both properties until you sell the third.

If your adjusted gross income exceeds $40,000 on a joint return and you or your spouse is covered by a pension plan at work, part of your IRA contributions may not be deductible. You must save your tax return and Form 5498 for each year you make nondeductible IRA contributions, until the funds are withdrawn. (Better build an addition to the garage.) And you will also want to keep records indefinitely for any year in which you pay alternative minimum tax in order to claim a credit in later years. Alternative minimum tax is an additional tax imposed if you claim certain deductions or credits that reduce or eliminate your regular tax.

Finally, keep copies of your tax returns forever. You may need to refer back to them in preparing subsequent returns if you have to pay alimony, sell business or investment property at a loss, or suffer a net operating loss. They show your progress, too, from struggling newlyweds to prosperous old-timers.

Simplify your taxes. According to the IRS, it takes 4 hours and 8 minutes to prepare a Form 1040 with itemized deduc-

no more attention than a corpse. Seven worry-free investments are discussed in Chapter 4, along with seven speedy investment techniques.

Asset management accounts. An asset management account does everything but whistle "Dixie." Bearing brand names, such as Merrill Lynch CMA and Schwab One, they combine a brokerage margin account with a money market account, a checking account, and a credit card. To top it all off, they track all your banking and securities transactions on a single statement. All for an annual fee of $100 or less.

Most asset management accounts offer free checking. Or you can use a debit or charge card to make purchases or withdraw cash at many banks. A debit card also lets you use automatic teller machines at thousands of locations worldwide. The amount you can borrow depends upon the market value of your securities.

Some accounts include true credit cards that allow you to finance purchases, charging interest on the unpaid balance. The amount you borrow comes from a bank, not the brokerage firm, and you pay high bank-card rates.

For a few dollars more, you can deposit your paychecks and have your fixed monthly bills paid automatically. Every transaction is shown on your monthly statement, or you can call toll-free, 24 hours a day, to check on your balance and lines of credit.

You can choose from taxable or tax-free funds, and in some cases, federally insured money market accounts. Deposits or withdrawals from these funds incur no sales commission. Dividends, interest, deposits, and proceeds from the sale of stock are invested either daily or weekly into the money fund of your choice.

What are the drawbacks? Generally, these accounts are a

high-stakes game. Minimum deposit requirements usually range from $5,000 to $25,000 in cash or marginable securities (that is, listed stock, many over-the-counter stocks and mutual funds, and corporate or government bonds). There is no minimum balance requirement once the account is opened, however.

They may also be a trap for the unwary, because most of them are margin accounts—your broker automatically extends you credit using your stocks, mutual funds, or bonds as collateral. Unless you monitor your statements closely, you might not even realize you've borrowed money.

Worse, there's no repayment schedule. You have to discipline yourselves to pay off the debt. Until you do, the interest mounts, although the rates are reasonable—.75% to 2.25% above the prime rate. Moreover, a decline in the market value of your securities may trigger a margin call if you've borrowed heavily.

You can avoid the pitfalls of a margin account by opening a cash-only account, which does not offer a credit line. But you give up overdraft protection.

One of the prime benefits of asset management accounts becomes apparent at tax time. They provide a year-end summary of your investment income and securities transactions. The most comprehensive include summaries of your deductible expenses and capital gains and losses as well.

MAKING THE MOST OF YOUR TIME

Who wants to come home to an adding machine? You've had a long day. All you want now are a hot bath, a cold drink, and a sitcom on TV.

I sympathize. But you must manage your time as well as

your money. That may mean curling up occasionally with an annual report instead of Tom Clancy. Set aside a couple of hours a week to tackle financial tasks. Then make it a habit, like jogging.

It's not enough to carve out time; you must also use it effectively. Don't reconcile your checkbook on your knee with paper airplanes whizzing by your ear. Set up a well-lighted home office in a quiet spot. If your only space is the kitchen table, clear it completely and put the area off-limits while you are working.

For speed, batch related activities. Write all of your checks on the first Sunday of the month, for example. Then drop them into your tickler file by mailing date. You don't want your efficiency to cost you interest.

List activities that need to be done, then work through the list, crossing off each job as it is completed. Update the list daily or weekly. Don't remove an item until you have seen it through.

Be decisive. Weigh the pros and cons of an investment thoroughly, but not *ad infinitum*. "The only thing worse than a bad decision is indecision," says Professor Brown. Curb your perfectionism—it robs you of time—and money.

Fight that other nemesis, procrastination, too. The time to get started is now. Or at least when you finish reading this chapter.

Adding Hours to the Day

It's an axiom of modern life: if you run out of land, build up. The same holds true for time. When all your spare moments are filled, your time may have to serve two purposes. Or you may have to lease more time by hiring someone else. Try these tactics for double-decking your day:

- Use the telephone whenever possible. If you are always on the road, install a car phone to keep in touch with your broker, apartment manager, and banker, as well as your office.
- Turn idle time to profit. Catch up on routine financial reading while waiting at your doctor's office. Watch business shows on television, or listen to financial books on tape during your commute. Convert your briefcase into a portable office, so wait times aren't wasted.
- Take advantage of 24-hour financial services. Choose a bank close to your home with a 24-hour hot line and automated teller machine. Buy and sell stocks through a 24-hour brokerage firm.
- Combine pleasure and profit. Attend investment seminars on board a cruise ship. Inspect rental and commercial properties while you're on vacation. Shop for antiques or art on a tour of Europe. (*Note:* Buy collectibles for enjoyment rather than for investment, unless you qualify as an expert. With luck, you will also turn a profit, but don't count on it as a key element in your financial plan.)
- Cash in on your hobbies. Writing, painting, stamp collecting, dog breeding—all have profit potential. If you play at it hard enough, your hobby may become a business one day.
- Subscribe to a financial news and stock quote service. For the price of a phone call, you can dial up daily reports and technical analysis of thousands of companies.
- Trade stocks from home. With a personal computer, financial software, and a modem, you can buy and sell stocks directly from a number of discount brokers and banks. Fidelity, Charles Schwab, Citibank, and Chase Manhattan all offer investor programs. Bear in mind

that you are strictly on your own when trading by computer. There is no stockbroker or financial adviser to review your decisions.

- Delegate to your children. Train and pay them to sort and add up canceled checks, for example, or to read stock tables and graph the rise and fall of your stocks' prices every week.
- Hire a professional. An army of stockbrokers, accountants, lawyers, tax preparers, and financial planners stands waiting to answer your cry for help. See "Buying Time" on page 42.

AUTOMATING YOUR INVESTMENTS

Want to take a big byte out of the time you spend managing your money? Put the power of the microchip to work for you. Not only can a computer free you from time-consuming tasks, it can increase your profits, too.

It's not R2D2, but a personal computer can be an impressive investment tool. It relieves you of menial and repetitive chores, such as manual calculation and record keeping. It manages your budget, figures your taxes, tracks and evaluates any type of investment, reduces risks, and provides instant access to an immense storehouse of financial data. You can buy software to help you pick stocks, mutual funds, bonds, and real estate.

A computer also lets you play the valuable game of "What if." For example, you can create several hypothetical portfolios and chart them before actually investing any of your hard-won money. Similarly, by comparing information about different investments, you can determine which pays the best total return. Or you can test the effects of a major purchase on your cash flow or compare buying versus leasing.

Before you get overexcited, remember that money management takes more than math. A computer may be Einstein, but it is not Solomon. It has no caution, self-discipline, or common sense. It can't pick surefire winners or protect you from a fondness for losers.

In fact, it can't function at all without numbers. That means sitting hunched over your keyboard for several hours or minutes a week. And each software program will take at least a day to learn.

Personal computers are expensive, too. Before you plunk down around $2,000, consider whether you really need your own machine. For instance, do you have access to a personal computer at work that you can use after hours? Or can you make a deal with a friend who owns a computer to supply investment software that you both can share?

If you prefer a computer of your own, weigh the cost against the value of your time and enhanced profit. Will you harness the computer's power to perform a wide range of financial tasks or will you only use it to balance your checkbook? Will a computer pay for itself by freeing you or your spouse to work extra hours each week? Will it return 5% to 10% more on your investments by enabling you to respond rapidly to changing market conditions and so assume more risk?

Do you have other uses for a computer? Will it help you in your job or your children with schoolwork? Finally, assess your temperament. Are you comfortable using a computer? Then by all means consider abandoning the manual methods of Dickens's day in favor of a computer.

Once you decide to automate, a good place to start is with your personal finances. Without money, you can't begin to invest. Managing your personal finances, therefore, should be done even if you have no immediate investment plans.

Cash and Budget Management

Of all the potential uses of your computer, none is more important than managing your cash and budgeting. A computer lets you track your assets and helps maximize the cash you have to invest by controlling your spending—essential for successful investing.

More than a dozen personal finance software packages are on the market. Most of them have moved well beyond checkbook balancing and now offer a complete financial record-keeping system.

One of the most comprehensive finance programs is *Andrew Tobias' Managing Your Money* (MECA, $219.98). Besides balancing your checkbook, it helps set up a household budget, estimates your income tax, analyzes stocks and bonds, assists with insurance and retirement planning, figures compound interest, and calculates your net worth. It also features a portfolio-management program.

Other programs combining some of the same features include *Dollars and Sense* (Monogram, $179.95), *Sylvia Porter's Personal Financial Planner* (Timeworks, $99.95), and *WealthBuilder* (Reality Technologies, $249.95).

If you want help only with budgeting and your checkbook, consider a program like *Quicken* (Intuit, $59.95). This program tracks your cash, checking account, and credit card balances, expenses, and net worth. It also prints checks, income and expense reports, and a tax summary.

Investment Evaluation and Selection

Following a dozen or more securities in various industries, each reacting differently to trends in inflation or interest rates, requires more than a pen and paper. Fortunately, there are many programs on the market that track stocks, bonds, mutual funds, options, and commodities.

With most of this software, you can compute the market value of your entire portfolio in a matter of minutes. You can even set prices at which you want to sell or buy shares, and your computer will alert you when it is time to act.

You can also screen securities for any market indicators or other traits you are seeking by subscribing to a data base, such as CompuServe. This on-line service can screen for favorable debt-to-equity ratios, price-book value, returns on sales, cash flow, and assets and equity. It can also compare a stock's current price to past performance or measure a stock's price fluctuations.

Other stock-screening services include *Compustock, Value/Screen Plus* (a condensed version of Value Line Investment Survey), and *Winning Investor.* Among the mutual fund software are *Mutual Fund Scoreboard* (Business Week, $299 to $399 per year), *Mutual Fund Investor* (American River Software, $149), *Fund Master-TC* (TimeTrend Software, $289), and *MetaStock* (Equis International, $349).

Each program reflects its designer's own theory or technique for selecting and managing securities. In choosing this type of software, ask the following:

- Do we understand and agree with the investment philosophy used?
- What indicators does the program analyze, and how can we use them to trade more profitably?

- Are the program's investment objectives consistent with ours?

Real Estate Analysis and Property Management

Real estate is the surest way to wealth. At least eighty-seven members of the Forbes 400 owe their fortunes to land and buildings. These tycoons employ a legion of assistants to search out and manage their properties. Luckily, you can rely on less expensive, but no less humble, resources. Several software programs help aspiring real estate moguls screen and select properties, while others tackle the job of managing your holdings.

Managing income property. Rental owners must collect rents, keep track of tenants' deposits, pay operating expenses and taxes, and make improvements. Property-management software takes charge of the tiresome record-keeping chores.

The best programs organize tenant files, record income and expenses, write checks to vendors, post rent checks to bank accounts, and track security deposits. They also report vacancies, delinquent tenants, and lease expirations. Two software packages for individual investors are *The Landlord Plus* (The Landlord's Software Center, $295) and *Basic Property Management* (Yardi Systems, $495).

Note: If you own only one or two rental properties, you may find that property-management software is too costly and bothersome. Buy a simple rental ledger at a stationery store instead.

Selecting properties. While some factors in real estate evaluation are subjective—for example, the desirability of a location—most involve the mathematical acrobatics that computers love. This makes it easy to analyze cash flow and to ask a variety of "what if" questions: What is the effect of the purchase price, down payment, interest rate, and mortgage term on your return of investment? What effect will raising rents 7% have on your cash flow? Is it better to take out a $10,000 second mortgage to buy a new roof or to spend $1,500 annually for the next 10 years to keep the old roof in repair?

For professional investors who want an in-depth evaluation, there is *Real Estate Analyzer* (HowardSoft, $395). *Managing Your Money* (MECA, $219.98) also includes simple property-analysis features.

Tax Preparation

Tax software can do away with the tedious sums, countless calculations, and math errors that make April so taxing. It lets you revise your return in seconds if you discover overlooked deductions or income. It allows you to experiment with different combinations of depreciation, expensing, and IRA contributions to save the most tax. Best of all, it frees you for the more lucrative task of tax planning, answering such questions as the tax consequences of buying or leasing a car, investing in rental property, or rolling over a pension plan distribution.

If you use short Forms 1040EZ or 1040A, however, you can prepare your return as efficiently and more economically with a calculator. Even if you file a regular Form 1040, you probably do not need a tax program if your return is fairly straightforward. But if you find yourself bogged down in such technical traps as depreciation, business schedules, partnership distributions, or five-year averaging, tax software may be a good investment.

Tax software performs two functions: (1) it stores and organizes your income and expense records and (2) provides you with this information to prepare your return or analyze tax strategies.

Financial record-keeping programs may be combined with a tax-preparation program. Not only are you getting more for your money with these programs, but you need to enter your financial data only once.

Make sure the program you buy incorporates the latest tax law. Find out whether the program is updated for changes or you must purchase a new program each year.

Leading tax-preparation programs include *Tax Preparer* (HowardSoft, $295), *Andrew Tobias's TaxCut* (MECA, $79.95), and *TurboTax* (ChipSoft, $75).

Information Services or Utilities

It is almost impossible to sift through, much less absorb, all of the financial data available these days. Subscribing to an information service, however, provides a rapid way to obtain data pertinent to your investment goals. For example, you may want recent stock prices for a certain industry. To achieve this, you can spend a lot of time doing manual research, or you can use a computerized information service.

Information services are electronic libraries. You subscribe by paying a one-time password fee. After that, your monthly bill depends on the number of hours you use the service.

Before choosing an information service, decide what kind of data you need. You can use these services for stock quotes, detailed historical pricing information, and information on the economic conditions underlying market trends, industries that are faring well, and specific stocks that look promising.

The major information services are Dow Jones/News Retrieval and CompuServe. Both provide current historical pricing, corporate statistics, earnings reports, stock quotes, and financial news.

On-line trading. You can buy and sell stocks from your home with an on-line discount brokerage service. Three information utilities offering this service are Dow Jones/News Retrieval, CompuServe, and Prodigy. Each utility orders through a particular brokerage firm, and you must open an account with that firm before trading. You can also trade on-line through Charles Schwab & Co. if you buy Schwab's *Equalizer* software.

BUYING TIME: HIRING PROFESSIONAL HELP

Like soybeans, time is a commodity. Don't expect to find it listed on the Chicago Board of Trade, though. Time has its own marketplace—the world of personal service. If you have the money, someone has the time. Time to cook your supper, walk your dog, scrub your floors. Time to help you decorate or pack up and move. And most important, time to manage your money, give legal advice, plan your estate, and prepare your tax return.

If you're so busy that your money is a victim of neglect, then buying the time of financial advisers may be your best investment. Even if you're not in the market for time, you may need the knowledge these experts have for sale. Almost everyone needs a lawyer, tax adviser, or insurance agent now and again.

Which advisers you need depends on your income, your net worth, the value of your time, and the complexity of your financial affairs. You probably shouldn't hire a financial planner, for instance, until your earnings are at least $50,000 and your net worth is at least $100,000. Snobbery has nothing to do with it. The planner's fees will offset the economic benefit of his advice if your wallet weighs less than that.

On the other hand, if each billable hour that you spend managing your money costs you $150, hiring an adviser for $100 is a bargain. This "it's-not-worth-my-time" argument only holds Perrier, however, if you would be actually earning $150. If you're taking two-hour lunches and killing the time between clients fiddling with executive toys, planning your investments won't really cost you a thing.

If you have unique business or investment interests, you may need specialized talent. If you collect art or antiques, for example, you may want to engage an appraiser; if you are an inventor, you need a patent attorney.

Deciding which kinds of advisers are right for you is the first small step. Now comes the impossible leap of picking the best. There are more advisers than extras in a Cecil B. DeMille epic. Many are well-trained professionals, but even more are self-styled experts with dubious credentials. Not to mention the outright con artists and frauds.

To add to the dilemma, there is no objective standard to measure one accountant's performance, for example, against another's. The best-represented client in a lawsuit can lose. And the track record of a stockbroker in the past is no guarantee of profits in the future. There's no warranty, either. You can't get your money back if your adviser is careless, crooked, or incompetent.

How can you ensure that *your* team is Super Bowl material? One of the most reliable ways is still word-of-mouth. Ask friends, relatives, or business associates in similar financial circumstances for recommendations. Or ask the financial professionals you already use.

You can also get referrals from professional organizations, such as your local bar association for lawyers or the International Association for Financial Planning or Institute of Certified Financial Planners for financial planners. And don't overlook the company where you work—the firm's lawyer, accountant, and banker may be an equally good choice for you.

Make a list of candidates and screen them by phone. Weed out advisers with less than five years' experience, those who show little or no interest in your problems, or those whose temperament doesn't match yours. Once you have narrowed your prospects to two or three, arrange a personal interview. Be sure to ask whether there is a fee for this preliminary meeting. If so, decide whether you are willing to pay for it.

Politely, but firmly, insist on a face-to-face meeting. Both you and your spouse should be present. The interview will usually last 15 to 20 minutes, so be prepared. Know exactly what questions you want to ask, and don't waste time on chit-chat.

What are you looking for? Besides such basics as credentials and fees, you are looking for such personal qualities as a reputation for integrity, an empathetic understanding of your needs, and a belief that every client is important.

Be alert for visual clues. Are files, books, and letters piled helter-skelter on every surface? Is there a stack of unreturned phone messages by his or her elbow? Does he or she dress professionally—and require the same of the staff? On the other hand, don't be overimpressed by the opulence of the office. The richness of the decor tells you more about the fees than the quality of the service. In fact, nearly every swindler hides behind a glittering facade.

The questions you ask depend in part on the type of advice you are seeking—legal, financial, or tax. But there are some questions you should ask *any* adviser or firm with whom you plan to do business:

- How long has the adviser or firm been in business?
- How large is the firm and in what areas does it specialize?
- What credentials does the adviser have? Does he or she belong to any professional organizations?
- What type of clientele does the firm represent—companies or individuals, large or small portfolios? Does its experience include clients in similar circumstances? Are client references available?
- Is this adviser willing to work with your other advisers?
- How are fees charged? By the hour? On a plan or project basis? Is a retainer required? Does the adviser also receive commissions from products he sells you? Are fees and commissions negotiable? If the fees seem too high, say so. One of my colleagues convinced his attorney to do his legal work for half the initially quoted fee.
- Will your agreement and estimated fees be put in writing?

If the adviser is reluctant to answer such questions or gives you vague or confusing answers, scratch that person from your list.

Once you have selected your advisers, encourage them to work together. Your stockbroker, for example, should consult your tax adviser about the impact of rolling over IRA accounts. Your estate lawyer should speak with your accountant before drawing up wills and trusts. All of them should coordinate strategy with your financial planner, who can be appointed as overseer. A major advantage of teamwork is that it serves as a system of checks and balances, protecting you from out-of-date, inaccurate, or self-serving advice.

No matter how brilliant or trustworthy your advisers, *never* surrender complete control of your finances. No one cares as much about your money as you do. Besides, your lack of interest or awareness makes you an easy mark for advisers who have their commissions, instead of your interests, at heart.

The only way to tell whether you have chosen wisely is to review their performance. Monitor work carefully for the first few months, then at set intervals. The most important measure is an adviser's success at meeting the goals for which he was hired. Other criteria include timeliness, the level of service, how well you are kept informed, and the professional appearance of correspondence and reports. If you are dissatisfied, find a new adviser.

Lawyer

Law touches every area of finance, from loans to taxes to wills. For this reason, you may need to hire more than one lawyer—one for real estate transactions, another for business ventures, and a third for estate planning.

You have plenty of choices—there are almost 750,000 lawyers in the United States. But first, ask whether you can handle the matter yourselves. Law is largely paperwork. You may be able to solve your problem by filing a complaint with a government agency, by using a legal form or preprinted contract, or by taking your case to Small Claims Court. You can also try negotiating a settlement yourselves or seek arbitration or mediation.

Even if you need professional help, most legal matters are routine enough to be handled by a legal clinic or an inexpensive legal chain, such as Jacoby & Meyers or Hyatt Legal Services. Fees are usually well below those charged by private practitioners.

Your employer or union may offer a prepaid legal plan as a fringe benefit. In those cases, for a flat annual fee of between $100 and $200, you have unlimited use of the group's lawyers for simple tasks, such as reviewing contracts. You receive a discount of up to 30% on a lawyer's hourly rate for more complicated cases.

You should seek the services of a skilled general practitioner or specialist if you need help in establishing a small business, arranging a tax-deferred exchange, resolving estate or tax problems involving substantial amounts of money or property, or preparing a complex will. Don't pay extra for the prestige of a big-name firm, though. Those partnerships charge up to $350 an hour.

Specific questions you should ask prospective lawyers are:

- What percentage of his practice is devoted to cases like ours? Ask about the results of similar cases, including the time spent and fees charged.
- Will he personally work on our case or delegate it to an associate? If it will be handled by an associate, will his services be billed separately at his lower rate? Take time to meet the associate at the end of the interview.
- How long will it take to complete the case, and what is his estimate of the cost?
- If you and your lawyer disagree, will he consent to binding arbitration? This can save you a tremendous amount of legal fees in the event of a dispute.

Have your lawyer draw up a retainer agreement. Ask that all fee arrangements and agreed-upon services be written in the contract. In addition, include a provision for settling any disputes, such as fee disagreements. Also, request a written estimate of all costs, including expenses. Ask that all bills be itemized and sent to you regularly. You may also want to set a ceiling on costs, which can be exceeded only with your written permission.

Tax Practitioner

Most people would rather come face-to-face with Jaws than with Form 1040. This fear isn't helped any by Congress, which unleashes "reform" every time you think it's safe to go back into the tax law.

If you can conquer your qualms, however, you may find that you can handle your taxes alone—as do some 14 million Americans who itemize. You can probably prepare your return yourselves if

- your income derives mainly from salaries;
- your write-offs are limited to the most common itemized deductions;
- you do not own rental property, your own business, or limited partnership interests;
- you did not sell your home or other investment property during the year.

If you want to file solo, buy an up-to-date tax guide. You may also want to call the IRS for a copy of its free Publication 17, *Your Federal Income Tax.*

If you decide to use a tax professional, you have four categories to choose from: certified public accountants (C.P.A.s), attorneys, enrolled agents, and unenrolled tax preparers.

A **C.P.A. or attorney** has specialized accounting or legal training and experience and therefore should be more knowledgeable about the tax law than other preparers who lack these credentials. Ask whether they specialize in taxes, however. Not all do. Even attorneys who do concentrate on taxes are usually more interested in tax planning and analysis than in filling out tax forms.

Attorneys and C.P.A.s are costly, too, charging from $100 to $200 an hour and up. If you are self-employed, however, you probably need the services of a C.P.A. If you are being pursued by the IRS, you want a tax lawyer.

An **enrolled agent** is a preparer who has worked for the IRS for at least five years or who has passed a rigorous two-day examination given by the IRS. An enrolled agent is authorized to practice before the IRS in an audit and can represent you at the Appellate level if your audit is appealed.

An enrolled agent often provides the same quality of tax preparation and planning as an attorney or C.P.A., but at 25% less cost. You can locate an enrolled agent by calling the National Association of Enrolled Agents at 800-424-4339.

The risk in hiring an **unenrolled tax preparer** is that in most states, he or she has no formal qualifications. For this reason, exercise extra care in selecting such a preparer. Many unenrolled preparers are retired persons or workers in other fields who prepare returns only during the tax season.

An unenrolled preparer often provides the advantage of reasonable fees. The fee for a short form is usually around $50; a Form 1040 with itemized deductions averages around $100. This buys you tax preparation, but no tax planning advice.

No matter which category of preparer you use, there are certain precautions you should take. First, beware the preparer who sets up shop in January, then closes his doors in April. Tax problems can occur at any time of the year. Make sure the preparer will be around if you are audited or queried by the IRS.

Request an estimate for preparing your return. If the fee

is based on an hourly rate, get an estimate of how long the work will take. Ask whether the preparer will pay the interest and penalties if he makes an error. And find out whether the preparer will represent you in an audit and whether there is an extra charge for this service.

Steer clear of any preparer who guarantees you a refund or whose fee is a percentage of your refund.

Also avoid any preparer who makes questionable suggestions, such as that you overlook an item of income, or who takes little or no time to find out the facts. A good preparer will explain the law or give you helpful hints to improve your record keeping or tax outlook.

Look for someone with your same tax temperament. Some people prefer conservative tax practitioners, while others favor aggressive advisers who will suggest write-offs that may be questioned by the IRS.

Never sign a blank return; always demand a copy of your return; and never allow the preparer to use his address on the top of the return so that your refund comes to him. Finally, the only way to ensure an accurate return is to review it thoroughly before signing. Don't be afraid to question items you don't understand, and insist on clear, convincing answers.

Stockbroker

Many people expect their brokers to be a combination of Michael Milken, Mother Teresa, and Kreskin. They are likely to be disappointed. The most a full-service broker can do is offer advice about strategies and recommend promising securities. His tips will not make you rich, however, unless luck and a bull market are on your side.

If you don't get that elusive trio mentioned above, you do get a trace of Dr. Jekyll and Mr. Hyde. While your broker wants his stock picks to add to your wealth, he also wants your stock trading to increase his commissions. You, therefore, have to approach a broker with a mixture of faith and distrust.

Of course, if you do your own research and are confident enough to choose your own stocks, you can avoid any conflict of interest by using a discount brokerage, such as Charles Schwab & Co., Rose & Co., or Quick & Reilly. Because discounters merely execute trades, you save up to 70% if you are buying or selling 500 shares or more. There are no savings on trades of 100 shares or less, however, because discounters charge a minimum fee per order.

If you don't have time to research stocks or simply want advice and camaraderie, then a full-service broker is for you. Look for a firm that has been in business for at least 10 years, is a member of the New York Stock Exchange, and belongs to the Securities Investor Protection Corporation (SIPC), which insures accounts for up to $500,000 if a brokerage fails.

Select at least three firms and set up a brief meeting with the branch manager to explain your investment needs. Tell the manager how much you have to invest and your goals— for example, you want to invest your $10,000 IRA for retirement and another $10,000 for your toddler's college education. Then ask the manager to recommend a suitable broker.

In your interview with the broker, ask him to define his investment approach clearly. Does his philosophy make sense, and more important, does it agree with yours? For example, if the broker says, "I put all my clients into small growth stocks," and you prefer blue chips, continue your search.

Find out what investment products the broker specializes in. These should be appropriate for your income and match your tolerance for risk. Be leery of the investments that are wildly speculative, such as penny stocks, commodities, and options, or which carry high commissions or fees, such as gold and real estate limited partnerships.

Make sure the broker knows what rate of return you expect and how you feel about taking risks. Stress that you want to be alerted not only when to buy, but when to sell—either after the stock has hit a targeted level or after an initial drop—in order to prevent further losses. If your portfolio is well diversified, request at least a quarterly performance review.

After the interview, verify the broker's credentials. He should be registered with the National Association of Securities Dealers. You can check this out by calling the state securities commission and asking to be read the broker's CRD file—the Central Registration Depository report that the broker must complete. This file tells how long a broker has been in business, where he has worked and for how long, and whether disciplinary actions have ever been brought against him.

Evaluate your broker's performance after the first six months and every three months thereafter. Use the prevailing rate of one-year T-bills for comparison. If you are not topping it—especially if you are taking high risks—you may want to look for another broker. Be fair, though. If the market crashed again in October, don't blame the decline on your broker.

Financial Planner

Think of your finances as a set of scales that must be delicately balanced. If you invest too heavily on the side of tax savings, favoring low income and deductions over higher income and appreciation, for example, your retirement fund will be underweight, or you'll be light on tuition when your namesake heads for college. If you put too much money into stocks, the scales may tip dangerously if the market plummets.

You can attempt this balancing act yourselves, or you can hire a financial planner. A financial planner is a master of the pie chart—advising you to put X% of your money in term-life insurance and Y% in mutual funds, for instance. He makes sure that all the scales—cash flow, debts, taxes, retirement, estate planning, and insurance—stay in equilibrium. He also sees to it that your investments are well diversified, to keep your yield steady if the economy shakes the scales.

A planner does not seize control of your finances, however. He drafts a written plan suggesting alternative investments to meet specific goals. A budget may also be included to help you save needed capital. Finally, you receive estate-planning advice.

Acting on this plan is up to you. Some people treat their plans like menus, following advice only when it agrees with decisions they have already made. Others shut theirs in a drawer and forget about them. Financial plans are only blueprints; you must be the builder.

A good time to find a suitable financial planner is when your family income or your investable assets exceed $50,000. Below that, the cost of hiring a planner—$500 to $5,000 in the first year—probably outweighs the economic benefit. Proceed with caution, however, because anyone can call himself a financial planner. More than 100,000 do. Only one in three is qualified.

Limit your search, therefore, to planners with certain credentials. A certified financial planner (C.F.P.) or a chartered financial consultant (Ch.F.C. or C.F.C.) must pass a series of exams and have three or more years' experience. A registered financial planner (R.F.P.) has passed state insurance and securities exams. Other initials that may be listed after a planner's name are C.F.A., chartered financial analyst, M.S.F.S., master of science in financial services, and the more easily recognized C.P.A., M.B.A., and J.D. (law degree).

If you demand the best, interview only members of the Registry of Financial Planning Practitioners. For a free list of registry members, write to the IAFP, 2 Concourse Parkway, Suite 800, Atlanta, GA 30328.

You can't judge a planner by his credentials alone, however. You must also consider fees. Cross off commission-only planners. Their advice is free because they earn their living from commissions on the investments and insurance they sell you. They may be sorely tempted to push products you do not need.

Fee-only planners do not sell anything. They charge a flat or hourly fee for their advice, your annual plan, and any periodic reviews. This objectivity does not come cheap. Expect to pay $1,500 to $5,000 in the first year and about half that in subsequent years. For this reason, many clients of fee-only planners have incomes of at least $100,000.

A fee-and-commission planner is more economical, with costs topping out at about $600 for the first year. Just remember that these planners are also salespeople—60% to 80% of their incomes is from commissions. You, therefore, have a right to ask your planner to justify his investment choices.

When you interview planners, ask about their backgrounds and experience. Many self-styled planners are stockbrokers or insurance agents in disguise. For confirmation, ask to see the ADV form that financial planners or their firms must file with the Securities and Exchange Commission. This states the planner's experience, how he is paid, whether he has a financial interest in the investments he sells, and whether he has been disciplined by regulatory agencies. Ask what rate of return you can expect in five years. A planner should outpace inflation by at least 4% or 5% a year. Also, request client references and a copy of a plan recently prepared for a client (the name will be blacked out for confidentiality). If the planner refuses, head for the door.

Evaluate your planner a year after you receive the written plan. Have you met your short-term goals? Are you making progress on your long-term ones? Have your investments yielded the desired level of return? Has your net worth increased? Do you feel secure? If so, congratulations. If not, don't hesitate to switch—there is no contract binding you.

Money Managers

Like chauffeurs and private jets, money managers are a mark of status and privilege. In the past, that was because most of the best managers wouldn't handle assets of less than $250,000 or $500,000. Even if you find one of the growing number today who will handle individuals with $50,000 or less to invest, the fees can make joining the elite unappealing. You can probably do equally well with a good mutual fund—which is run by a specialized money manager.

Money managers usually charge an annual fee of 1% to 2% of your account's assets, with a minimum fee of $800 to $1,000. In addition, you pay the brokerage commissions when your manager trades stocks or bonds on your behalf. These can run from 1% to 2% of your assets in the first year, when the manager must buy a complete portfolio. In subsequent years, they drop about a quarter of a percent. If you have less than $50,000, the combined management fee and commissions could consume up to 4% of your holdings.

What services does a money manager provide? Unlike the

financial planner, who helps you define your financial goals, a manager is an investment specialist who takes charge of your portfolio. In most cases, you sign an agreement permitting him or her to trade for your account without asking you first. If you can't sleep while a stranger is juggling your nest eggs, a money manager is not for you.

Money managers are found at brokerage firms and bank trust departments. Others work for small, independent investment advisory firms controlling between $50 million and $500 million. Ask for referrals from your financial planner, broker, or accountant.

Don't fall for the manager with the flashiest track record. Too often, statistics are inflated, with managers using mirrors to make their numbers look better than they are. Beware, for example, the manager who uses "model" accounts to report performance. These hypothetical accounts don't exist and are no proof of actual performance. No better is the "representative account" that is actually the manager's best performer.

Ask the manager for a report that reflects a composite of all accounts he has carte blanche to run. The total return should be net of management fees and calculated on a time-weighted basis.

Compare the manager's record year by year with an index, such as Standard & Poor's 500 stock index. Not even first-rate managers can be expected to beat this index every year, but they should be able to show superior results over a period of five years or more.

Finally, request a copy of the ADV form the manager filed with the Securities and Exchange Commission. This form discloses information about the manager's education, experience, fees, and investment strategy. It also reveals whether the manager or firm has been disciplined by the

SEC or other regulatory agencies. Then ask for the phone numbers of at least three clients.

Don't hire a money manager until you decide your investment goals, including your desired rate of return and maximum risk tolerance. Then, working with the manager, write into the client agreement a set of guidelines for managing your account. For example, you might state that your portfolio should outperform rates on long-term certificates of deposit by at least three percentage points, net of all fees. Or that you must be consulted before the manager buys over-the-counter stock.

Evaluate your manager's performance with each quarterly statement. If you have losses, ask the manager to explain them and to tell you what he is doing to correct them. Once a year, review how well your manager has met your goals, how well he did compared to the markets in which your money was invested, and whether you could have done almost as well with a money market or mutual fund.

4

FAST MONEY:
The Busy Two-Earner
Investment Guide

If you have seen the future, you know it is lived in double time. You will watch split-screen TVs, conduct business while you commute, and complain if your microwave doesn't have dinner sizzling 8.6 seconds after you walk in the door. You will try to make one lifetime do the work of two, or you will be hauled into court and fined $500 for the new crime of wasting time.

For most two-earner couples, the future is now. You are already leading a double life—snatching minutes from busy careers to manage your finances. You need to be one-minute money managers, because that's all the time you've got.

This chapter shows you how to invest your money, not your time. There are trade-offs, however. Money does not microwave. You can't expect the highest yields from the least personal involvement. But you don't have to settle for a passbook pittance, either. The hard-working investments and investing techniques discussed below can give you the best of both goals.

Don't feel limited to the investments here. They are recommended for their lack of fuss, to overcome the restraints of time, and to get you started. Then, if you find time, you can branch out into more diverse and potentially more profitable ventures. I think you'll discover that investing can be as habit-forming as any stimulant, especially as your wealth begins to multiply, opening up more and greater investment doors. Then the investments you choose will depend solely on your objectives and tolerance for risk.

In fact, your investment strategy should change through the years. The aggressive stance you adopt in your 20s should probably become more conservative as you approach retirement. In the second half of this chapter, therefore, we explore investment choices for every stage of your life.

Before you embark on your investment career, however, there are certain steps every couple should take to ensure their financial security. These 10 investment "musts" are found at the end of the chapter.

No matter what direction your investing takes, it's important to begin NOW. Ironically, the best time-saver is time itself. If you invest $10,000 today at 8%, your money will double in just nine years. Without your lifting a prospectus. Wait and you have to do the hard work yourselves.

SEVEN SPEEDY INVESTMENTS

The problem with high-flying investments is that they may suddenly take a nosedive. You don't dare leave the cockpit or glance up from the instrument panel. Busy investors risk having their financial plans crash and burn before reaching their destinations.

You need investments that you can trust on automatic pilot. The following vehicles will fly safely within minutes after you get them off the ground. You only have to pop back in once a year to review your portfolio for performance and tax consequences. If an investment has strayed off its desired course, take up another one on the list.

1. EE Savings Bonds

Once purchased for patriotism, not profit, Series EE savings bonds have shed their amateur status, targeting the sophisticated investor with fairly competitive, variable rates. Even so, owners of savings bonds are still thought of as more Walter Mitty than Douglas Fairbanks. But it's precisely that simplicity and safety that make these bonds ideal investments for two-earners on the go.

If it's a matter of pride, tell your buddies that your money is perilously invested in some swashbuckling enterprise. But put your money in bonds. Issued and backed by the federal government, there is no safer investment. Sold at 50% of face value (a $1,000 bond costs $500, for instance), EE bonds pay a variable interest rate that is adjusted every six months. This means they keep step with inflation. After five years, they pay 85% of the average market yield of five-year Treasury securities, or 6%, whichever is greater. (However, bonds held less than five years earn interest at fixed, graduated rates that begin at 4.16%.)

EE bonds are tax fighters, too. All interest is exempt from state and local taxes. Federal taxes can be deferred until the bonds are cashed in or mature. Even at maturity, you can keep the IRS from your door still longer by rolling your bonds over into Series HH bonds. The accumulated interest does not have to be reported until the HH bonds mature or are cashed in. The HH bonds pay interest semiannually, though, and taxes are due on this amount.

Savings bonds need less maintenance than Mount Rushmore. Stash them someplace fireproof. That's it. You don't have to worry about reinvesting your earnings, because EE bonds don't pay current interest. You receive your accrued interest when you cash in the bond for its full face value.

Saving for the future is easy with EE bonds. They can be timed to mature when your child enters college, for example, or when you reach retirement age. In fact, bonds bought after 1989 will pay tax-free interest if you use them for your child's college tuition. *Note:* Interest will be fully nontaxable only for parents with joint adjusted gross incomes of $60,000 or less. See Chapter 9 for details.

Don't buy bonds if you will need the money within six months. Bonds can't be redeemed during that period.

The fastest way to buy bonds is from your bank, savings and loan, or credit union. Or sign up for an automatic savings plan where you work. To avoid long lines, order by mail by writing to the Bureau of Public Debt, Parkersburg, WV 26106-1328. Before investing, call 800-US-BONDS to check on the current interest rate.

2. Certificates of Deposit

If you agree to surrender your money for a specified period of time, ranging from six months to five years or longer, your reward is a higher interest rate than banks offer on their savings or money market accounts. However, once the bank has your money, it all but throws away the key. You will incur a substantial penalty if you cash in your certificate early.

Your time is required here for two decisions. First, you must choose between a fixed or variable interest rate. Next comes the question of how long to tie up your money. If you believe interest rates are near their high or about to fall, lock into a two-year CD. If you think rates will climb even higher, buy a shorter-term certificate so your money will be free to reinvest as interest rises. What if you haven't a clue whether rates will go up, down, or sideways? Buy several CDs with different maturities. As each one matures, reinvest in a higher-yielding CD if rates have climbed or in another investment if rates have fallen.

Check your newspaper's financial pages for the bank offering the highest rate in your area. Or call several local banks and brokerage firms and compare rates. Ask the bank to send you an application form. Many banks let you buy CDs through the mail.

3. Money Market Mutual Funds

If yield, liquidity, and safety rank high on your list, it's hard to top money market mutual funds. In essence, money funds are mutual funds that invest solely in short-term debt securities, such as Treasury bills, commercial paper, and certificates of deposit. Tax-free money funds buy short-term municipal bonds whose interest is exempt from federal income tax.

Unlike stock and bond mutual funds, the price of money funds does not fluctuate. There is no risk of loss if the stock market goes haywire.

The interest rate paid by a money fund varies daily depending on its portfolio and the cost of money. Money funds usually pay higher rates than bank money market funds. Your dividends can be automatically reinvested in more shares. In choosing a money fund, look at its yield over the past 12 months.

The minimum initial investment is usually $1,000 to $5,000. You can add to your account or withdraw money at any time without penalty or a charge. Most funds offer unlimited check-writing privileges, as long as each check is for $500 or more. There is no minimum balance requirement once the account is open. Nor does the interest rate fall if your balance drops below a certain amount.

With money funds, you have the luxury of dealing by phone or by mail. For maximum timesaving, invest in a money fund that belongs to a family of funds. On the application form, check the box permitting you to transfer money from your fund to another fund in the group simply by lifting the telephone. Also sign up for wire transfers, to wire withdrawals directly to your bank account.

If you are in a high tax bracket, you may earn more, after taxes, with a tax-exempt money fund. For investors in the 28% bracket, a tax-exempt fund with a yield of 5% offers the equivalent of a taxable yield of 6.94% (7.46% in the 33% bracket).

If you live in a state with high income tax, such as New York or California, invest in a fund that buys only municipal bonds issued by your state. Your earnings are thus triply exempt—from federal, state, and local taxes.

To invest, call a fund's toll-free number, and ask for a prospectus and application form. You can also set up a money fund with your stockbroker. If you trade securities, this is a useful place to keep cash between buying and selling.

4. U.S. Treasury Issues

Want in on a secret? There's an investment that pays competitive rates, provides tax benefits, needs no research, and is as safe as the federal government (sorry, didn't mean to scare you).

Seriously, the government issues three virtually risk-free securities besides EE bonds—Treasury bills, bonds, and notes. All income from these securities is exempt from state and local taxes (but not federal tax). This feature can boost your after-tax yield on Treasuries above those of bank CDs or money market funds if you live in a high-tax state.

Treasury bills, priced at $10,000, are sold at a discount and redeemed at face value on maturity. The interest you earn is deducted from the purchase price. T-bills mature in 3, 6, and 12 months.

Sold in $1,000 and $5,000 denominations, **Treasury notes** mature in 1 to 10 years and pay a fixed rate of interest twice a year. The longer the note's maturity, the higher the interest rate. **Treasury bonds,** which mature in 10 to 30 years, can be bought for $1,000. They also pay interest twice a year.

Although Treasury securities are easily sold, you run the risk of loss if you are forced to sell notes and bonds prematurely. That's because a steep rise in interest rates can drive the price of your securities down before maturity. Don't use your emergency cash reserve to buy T-notes and T-bonds, therefore. T-bills, on the other hand, are more liquid because their rates are short-term and fluctuate less.

The speediest way to buy is through your stockbroker or bank. Expect to pay $25 to $50 for the convenience, however. If you have more time to spare, save the fee by buying directly from a Federal Reserve Bank or the Bureau of Public Debt (Washington, DC 20239).

If you prefer the mails, you can submit a tender offer form through the Federal Reserve Bank or one of its local branches, or through the Bureau of Public Debt, Securities Transaction Branch, Washington, DC 20226. Fill out the form and enclose payment for the full face amount. Pay with a certified personal check, cashier's check, a Treasury security redemption check, or Treasuries you own that will mature by the new issue date. State that you are making a noncompetitive bid, meaning that you will accept the average auction price.

Check current interest rates by calling the Bureau of Public Debt at 202-287-4088.

For more information, send for a booklet entitled "Buying Treasury Securities at Federal Reserve Banks" (Federal Reserve Bank of Richmond, Public Services Dept., Box 27622, Richmond, VA 23261; $4.50).

5. Blue-chip Stocks

Blue chips are the aristocracy of stocks. Like old money, they have staid and venerable reputations to maintain. They can be trusted with the long-term care of your capital. A brief glance at stock prices every few months is all that's necessary.

Blue-chip companies have long, proven earnings records, an unbroken history of paying quarterly cash dividends for 25 years or more, stable management, and low debt. These well-known companies include American Express, A.T.&T., Bristol-Myers, Coca-Cola, Dow Chemical, Du Pont, General Electric, General Motors, Kodak, 3M, Sears, and Westinghouse.

Besides paying dividends, blue chips have excellent capital gains potential. These are not hotshot growth stocks, however, so don't expect overnight profits. These low-risk stocks generally take time to appreciate.

Before investing, study the company's annual report, its *Value Line* or *Standard & Poor's* listing at your library, and the 52-week high and low shown in your newspaper's financial pages.

Buy blue chips through your stockbroker. If you already know which companies you want to buy, use a discount broker and save 50% to 75% on commissions. Extra shares can usually be added through a dividend reinvestment plan (see Investing Technique #7 on page 73).

6. Stock Mutual Funds

If you want a stake in American business, but you're too busy to research and choose your own stocks, invest in a mutual fund. A mutual fund is a company that pools money from thousands of investors to buy and sell securities. You buy shares in the fund, making you a part owner of its portfolio and entitling you to a portion of its earnings.

In the game of one-upmanship, mutual funds are clear winners over individual stocks. Their major advantages:

- Full-time professional management—the fund's stocks are monitored daily and buy-sell decisions are made, sparing you the work.
- Diversification—your money is spread among the hundreds of securities the fund owns, so a plunge in the price of one holding causes scarcely a ripple in the value of your investment.
- Minimal paperwork—you receive reports and earnings from only one company.
- Liquidity—selling your mutual fund shares is generally quick and easy.
- Variety—whether you seek income or growth, prefer health care over technology, or favor the Southwest over the Northeast, there is a fund for you, roughly 2,100 in all.

Diversification is a cushion, but no guarantee against a fall. The price of mutual fund shares fluctuates just as stocks do. In the October 1987 crash, the average stock mutual fund plummeted 20.9%, almost as much as the market as a whole.

You can buy into most funds for as little as $1,000. Some have no minimum at all. Once you are a shareholder, you can usually add more shares for a minimum $100 investment. Or you can sign up for automatic reinvestment of your dividends. Count on putting in two hours a month managing each fund.

Plan to hold your mutual fund shares for at least five years, to give your fund time to rebound from any downturns. If you think you might need the money sooner, stick to low-risk funds.

For convenience, invest in a family of funds—an investment company that operates several stock, bond, and money market funds as a group. Among the better-known fund families are Dreyfus, Fidelity, Putnam, T. Rowe Price, and Vanguard. You can move your money within the family, switching from one fund to another if the market dives or you decide to change your strategy from income to growth.

No-load mutual funds are bought directly from the management company by mail. For this reason, you pay no sales charges. Load funds are sold by stockbrokers and financial planners, who collect a sales charge of between 4% and 8.5% of your initial investment. Studies have shown that no-load and load funds perform equally well. It is, therefore, only worth investing in a load fund if, after research, you decide that fund best meets your investment goals.

In choosing a fund, determine whether you want income or growth and how much risk you are willing to assume. Select several funds that match your goals, and call or write for each fund's prospectus. Study the table showing the fund's operating expenses. As a rule, avoid funds whose operating expenses exceed 1.5% of their assets. You can get a list of most funds and their phone numbers from The Investment Company Institute, 1600 M Street NW, Washington, DC 20036. Or watch for the lists of funds published in *Barron's, Money,* or *Forbes.*

Look at a fund's total return, not its current yield. Total return takes into account fluctuations in the fund's share price. If a fund yields an impressive 15%, but the price dropped 12%, its total return to investors is a meager 3%. Compare a fund's 5- and 10-year track records with other funds sharing the same objective.

7. Single-premium Life and Universal Life II Insurance

These modern types of life insurance provide an effortless way for the busy investor to build up tax-deferred earnings. Because they are primarily investment vehicles, the insurance coverage is minimal. Don't buy either of these types of policies to meet your life insurance needs.

With single-premium life, you make a lump-sum premium payment, which ranges from $5,000 to $500,000. Most of your premium is invested, while a small portion goes toward insurance coverage. The income the policy earns is tax-deferred.

Universal Life II lets you make premium payments over time. You can choose how much money you want to pay in each year and the amount of the death benefit, within limits.

Both types of insurance guarantee a minimum rate of return on their cash value, usually around 4%. The company lets you decide where to invest your principal—in stocks, bonds, or money market mutual funds.

Single-premium life is an excellent way to borrow. You can generally borrow up to 75% of the cash value during the first year and up to 90% thereafter. Although the insurer charges an interest rate of around 8%, the actual cost of borrowing is zero. That's because the interest on the loan is considered equal to your return on the amount borrowed.

If you borrow, you don't get off tax-free, however. The amount of cash you borrow or withdraw from your policy is taxed to the extent of policy earnings. You are also subject to a 10% penalty on loans or withdrawals before age 59½, unless you become disabled.

A word of caution: Be sure you understand the sales charges. These run as high as 9% and can drastically reduce or even eliminate your return if you cash in the policy early. Beware, too, of high surrender charges if you take your money out during the first 7 to 10 years. If you do let the policy lapse, all the interest it has earned becomes immediately taxable.

Before investing, call several insurance companies, and read their literature carefully. Find out the **net** interest rate, that is, the return after deducting both the cost of insurance coverage and administrative expenses. Invest only with a company that has an A or A+ rating from A. M. Best Company.

Tax benefits are the major appeal of these types of insurance. Returns tend to be lower than with other investments.

SEVEN QUICK INVESTING TECHNIQUES

Investing can be like fine dining, rich, leisurely, and professionally served. For the busy investor, however, investing needs to be like the Automat—cheap, quick, and self-serve. The following techniques are to saving and investing what fast food is to eating out.

1. Automatic Payroll Deduction Plans

These plans make saving as effortless as breathing. Part of your paycheck is spirited away before you ever lay eyes on it and is invested in an IRA, money market fund, savings account, or EE savings bonds. You decide the amount and how often you want it deducted.

If your employer doesn't offer such a program, banks and credit unions do. Take a few minutes to fill out an authorization form, and the bank will deduct a set amount from your checking account on a day you name, such as the first of the month. Banks also automatically transfer funds from checking into a money market or savings account. Some banks allow transfers to a mutual fund, usually without charge.

If you belong to a credit union at work, a portion of your paycheck can be deposited automatically into your share account.

2. Deferred Pay (401)k Plans

If your employer offers a 401(k) plan, pump every nickel you can into it. Why? First, your contribution is nontaxable. It isn't even included in wages on your Form W-2. Second, your earnings grow tax-deferred. Finally, most employers boost employee morale by matching 25% to 100% of an employee's contribution.

The maximum you can contribute is $8,475 a year (indexed for inflation). Matching contributions by your employer can bring the total up to the lower of $30,000 or 25% of your salary.

This is a retirement savings plan. You may not withdraw funds until you reach age 59½, or you will be slapped with a 10% penalty. Exceptions: you leave the company, become disabled, or show economic hardship. Tax on a withdrawal can be deferred by rolling it over into an IRA account within 60 days.

You will be offered three or more investment options. Common choices include stock funds, bond funds, money market funds, guaranteed investment contracts (sponsored by insurance companies), and your employer's stock. As a general rule, no more than 10% of your retirement savings should be invested in your company's stock.

3. Company Profit-sharing Plans

If investing so much time at the office leaves you no time to invest, take advantage of your company's own pension or profit-sharing plan. After all, your efforts contribute to the profits. Why shouldn't your time investment pay as well as an investment of money?

Company plans vary widely, but they all offer a fast and easy way to invest. Ask your personnel office for details.

A profitable company may distribute a portion of its earnings to employees. Invest any profits you receive directly in one of the seven speedy investments recommended above. If your company holds your share of the profits in a trust, you don't have to make even an elementary investment decision.

Many profit-sharing plans let you make voluntary contributions, often matched by your employer. Earnings are tax-deferred. Don't contribute, however, until you know how well the plan or trust has performed, how much you can put in each year, how much is matched, and what restrictions there are on withdrawals.

No matter how convinced you are that your company is the next IBM (or even if it *is* IBM), never place all your investment bets on that one company. Protect yourself from your company falling on hard times by diversifying.

4. Employee Stock Purchase Plans

There's one stock you don't have to research—your employer's. Companies often let employees buy stock at bargain prices. Over the years, the rewards can be staggering. My great-uncle began working for Standard Oil when that company was in its infancy. Each year he duly bought the stock offered to employees. Even after the 1929 Crash, he retired a wealthy man.

The amount you decide to invest is automatically deducted from your paycheck. Most companies require you to contribute at least 1% of your salary to the plan.

You are not taxed on any gain or loss until you sell the stock.

5. Company Savings Plans

With these plans, you authorize your employer to invest part of your salary in a stock or bond mutual fund. Your employer may match your contribution. Your savings grow tax-deferred until the money is withdrawn.

Each company plan has different restrictions. Ask how much you may invest, the amount your employer will match, whether you must be vested to tap your savings, and the tax consequences.

6. Dollar-cost Averaging

Don't waste time waiting for the perfect moment to jump in and buy stock. Use a simple investing technique called dollar-cost averaging. You invest a fixed amount, say $100, every month, whether the price of the shares you're buying is going down or up.

What's the benefit? Over the long term—5 or 10 years— you are likely to acquire more shares at median, rather than high, prices. For example, $100 will buy 10 shares at $10 per share and 20 shares at $5 per share. You end up with 30 shares at an average price of $6.67.

Dollar-cost averaging works best with no-load mutual funds. It's not economical for individual stocks because the commission on a small purchase takes too big a bite out of your profits. And trading odd lots (under 100 shares) is even costlier.

The easiest way to use dollar-cost averaging is to arrange an automatic transfer between your bank and a mutual fund. The same amount of money is withdrawn on a specified date every month and transferred to the fund of your choice.

If dollar-cost averaging becomes too unexciting for you, experiment. For instance, increase the level of your investment as share prices fall and decrease it as prices rise. Or use more than one fund. In a bull market, invest your fixed amount in an aggressive growth fund. Switch to a growth and income fund in uncertain periods. And head for a straight income fund if the stock and bond markets take a prolonged downturn. A family of funds is handiest if you want to pursue this strategy.

7. Dividend Reinvestment Plans

One of the laziest ways to build a portfolio is through automatic dividend reinvestment. About a thousand companies let you invest your quarterly dividends in additional shares, sometimes at a 3% to 5% discount and usually without brokers' commissions.

Many companies also let you buy even more shares by

investing another $10 to $5,000 on top of your reinvested dividend, again bypassing a broker.

To participate, naturally you must own a company's stock. How many shares varies. In some plans one share is enough; others require 50 or 100. Don't sign on unless you plan to hold the shares long-term.

Reinvested dividends are taxable, just as if you had received them in cash. The tax is based on the fair market value of the stock on the dividend payment date. *Note:* Keep *every* single statement you receive from the plan. You will need them to determine your basis in the stock when you sell it.

You can obtain a list of companies offering dividend reinvestment plans by sending $2 to Public Relations Dept., Standard & Poor's Corporation, 25 Broadway, New York, NY 10004.

INVESTMENTS FOR THE TIMES OF YOUR LIFE

Couples pass through cycles, not of the seasons, but of marriage, the birth and emancipation of children, retirement, and the death of each spouse. At each stage, money adds to the texture, durability, and enjoyment of family life. And at each stage, money is servant to different goals.

Your investment strategy should shift with these cycles, reflecting the fresh concerns, priorities, and desires that each new phase brings. The purpose of this section is to help you manage your money and to select the investments best suited to your family's needs at every stage of your financial life span.

Getting Started

If you've only just begun, you have the most powerful wealth builder of all—time. Begin investing $2,000 a year at age 25 in an IRA earning 9% annual interest, and you can retire at age 65 with $738,584. Wait until you are 35 to begin, and you wind up with only $299,150.

It's crucial, therefore, to begin saving. How much doesn't matter, as long as you invest the same amount regularly. Aim to set aside at least 5% of your combined salaries.

Don't speculate. You are trying to establish a sound financial base. Concentrate on safe, simple investments, such as total return mutual funds (which invest for a combination of capital gains and interest or dividends) and money market mutual funds. Steer clear of investments that tie up your money for years or that you cannot cash in without penalty. The expenses of setting up a household, establishing a career, and eventually buying a house, require that your assets be liquid.

Establish credit and protect it. Don't abuse consumer credit—pay off credit card balances as they become due.

Begin saving for retirement by contributing to your employer's 401(k) plan or an IRA if there is no pension plan where you work. Put in only as much as you can afford to part with until you are age 59½.

Review the fringe benefits your employer offers. Decide whether to buy health insurance separately through your respective jobs or to be covered as a family under the more comprehensive of your two plans.

Hire a lawyer to draw up simple wills leaving everything to your surviving spouse.

This is a learning period. During these early years, ground yourselves in the basics of money management, study investments, and practice investing on paper or with computer investment games. Begin to define your own investment philosophy and to establish a long-range financial plan.

Beginning a Family

At this stage, you probably want to put down roots. The tax advantages and long-term investment potential make homeownership your top priority. Invest a portion of your savings in a starter home (see Chapter 6). Consider mortgage insurance so your new home can be paid off if one earner dies.

If you dream of starting your own business, do it now. You're not yet too firmly entrenched in someone else's enterprise, and you have enough years ahead of you to weather the inevitable setbacks and build a substantial fortune.

Take advantage of your employer's tax-deferred savings plans. Increase your contributions to your 401(k) plan or IRA. Join your company's stock purchase plan.

As your salaries rise, gradually increase your savings until you are putting aside 8% to 10% of your gross income each year. Cut back on recreation and indulgence purchases to free cash for key goals.

Shift half of your savings into growth stock mutual funds that outperform the market averages. Keep the balance of your portfolio in a total return mutual fund, money market mutual fund, or certificates of deposit. You still need liquidity to meet housing and child care expenses.

Begin planning for your child's education. The earlier you start, the less that you'll have to sock away each month. If you start saving $150 a month upon the birth of your child and invest the money at 7%, for example, you will have enough to pay the entire cost of your baby's B.A. at a public college when he or she turns 18. But wait until your child is

12 to start, and you will have to almost double your monthly savings.

Set up a custodian account under the Uniform Gifts to Minors Act for each child. Buy EE savings bonds or zero-coupon bonds that mature when your child enters college.

Buy term life insurance to ensure the financial security of your children if one or both of you dies. Do not purchase insurance on the life of your child. Review your existing health and disability coverage to see if it is adequate in light of changed circumstances.

Update your wills to name a personal guardian for your children and to name them as heirs if both of you die in a common accident. Add a testamentary trust to hold and manage your children's property. A testamentary trust is one that is created by your will to hold and distribute the income and property of your estate.

Trading Up—The Middle Years

Now is the time to capitalize on the financial base you have worked so hard to build. Your resources may be strained, however, by the expense of college and caring for elderly parents. And for the first time, you must squarely confront your own retirement.

Use the equity in your first home to trade up to a larger property. To save taxes, expand your real estate holdings to include at least one rental property.

Look for other ways to save on taxes. Continue to take advantage of tax-deferred savings plans. Shift income to your children over the age of 14, for example, by putting up to $20,000 per year into custodian accounts or by hiring them to work in your business. If you are self-employed, plow profits back into your business to increase revenue and to generate deductions.

Expand and diversify your portfolio. Save at least 15% of your income. Take advantage of your good credit to seize outstanding business or investment opportunities.

Invest college funds in total return mutual funds, money market mutual funds, or single-premium life insurance, depending upon the age of your child (see Chapter 9).

Retirement planning comes to the forefront. During this early phase, your goal is growth. This calls for aggressive investing. Put 70% of your retirement funds in growth stock mutual funds. If you are saving through your company-sponsored retirement plan, choose the equity or growth fund.

At this stage, you have the capital to invest in individual stocks. You need at least $12,000 to put together a minimally diversified portfolio of four or five stocks. Consider light blue chips—leading medium-sized companies with a steady rise in earnings over the last 10 years or more.

The remaining 30% of your retirement portfolio should go into safe, high-yield cash equivalent investments, such as money market mutual funds, Treasury bills, and short-term bank certificates of deposit. In company-sponsored plans, try money market funds and guaranteed investment contracts (sort of an insurance company CD).

For the best returns, stick to your chosen mix of investments until you enter the next stage of your retirement planning. Realign your portfolio once a year to keep your portfolio mix constant. For example, if a bull market pushes the value of your growth stock from 70% to 80% of your retirement fund, sell some of your shares to bring the value of your growth stock back down to 70%. Add the proceeds to your cash investments to restore them to 30% of your holdings.

Finally, increase your home insurance (if necessary), add

coverage for any collectibles, and consider buying an umbrella policy to supplement your liability coverage.

Peak Earning Years

As you reach the summit of your professions, don't hesitate to enjoy the rewards. Lavish some of your high earnings on yourself. You deserve it.

Increase your savings to 20% of your income. A shift in your investment mix is necessary, however, as you near retirement. You have more to lose and less time to recoup your losses. Gradually decrease your stock holdings by 20%, and move into high-quality bonds, mutual bond funds, or Treasury issues. Funds that invest in high-quality bonds—corporate or municipal bonds rated BBB or better or Treasuries—with maturities between 4 and 10 years generally provide the best balance between risk and gain.

Switch half the money you have in growth funds to shares in total return funds that hold bonds and cash as a cushion for their stock investments during bear markets. In company-sponsored plans, these are usually identified as equity income, or balanced, funds.

If you are selecting your own individual stocks, you might want to change your emphasis to traditional blue chips. Choose those with dividends that exceed the market average, because they have the best potential for long-term growth, even during market slumps.

Continue your real estate investment program. Purchase a second home, using a home-equity loan to finance the down payment, if necessary. Add a small multi-unit apartment building to your holdings.

As your children enter the homestretch for college, look into federal and state aid programs, scholarships, and commercial loans. Consider borrowing from your 401(k) plan to pay for education expenses. Generally 401(k) loans must be repaid within five years, with payments of principal and interest every three months. Your borrowing is limited to $50,000.

Reevaluate your life insurance needs. With the children almost fully grown, you may be able to decrease your coverage. Although it may seem premature, consider long-term-care insurance to cover nursing home costs in later years. Premiums are relatively modest when you are in your 50s, but by the time you reach 70, the cost may be prohibitive.

Retirement

With retirement comes a shift from acquiring to preserving assets. You probably want to reduce the number of your investments, consolidate your holdings, and increase liquidity by beginning to sell off your real estate. You may prefer to trade down to a smaller, more easily maintained home, and to add your gain to your retirement fund. You may exclude up to $125,000 of the gain from the sale of your home if you are age 55 or older and you used the home as your principal residence for at least three out of the five years before the sale.

How much should you have saved for retirement? Most folks need about 70% of their annual preretirement income to maintain the same standard of living. To estimate the amount of savings you need, subtract your anticipated social security and pension benefits from the annual income you'll require. Any remainder must come from savings. For example, suppose you estimate that social security and pension benefits will leave you $20,000 short of a comfortable annual income. If your assets are invested at 10%, you'll need savings of $200,000 to make up the shortfall without dipping into your capital.

Your employee-benefits department can estimate the size of your pension at retirement. For a projection of your future social security benefits, call 1-800-937-2000, or stop by your local Social Security office, and ask for Form SSA-7004.

Generally, if you managed to save 10% of your pretax earnings regularly from your 30s on, you can retire worry-free.

Traditionally, retirees shift their savings into safe, high-yielding income investments, such as Treasuries or certificates of deposit. This conservative urge is understandable, but it exposes you to the corrosive effects of inflation. For example, $400,000 invested in a Treasury bond yielding 8% simple interest will earn $32,000 a year. But after just 10 years of 5% inflation, that income will buy less than $20,000 does today.

The solution is to keep half of your savings in total return funds or blue-chip stocks. Of your remaining funds, 20% should be invested in high-grade bonds or bond funds, and 30% should be kept in cash-equivalent investments, such as money market funds or CDs.

After age 75, inflation ceases to be a concern. Trim your stock holdings to 40% of your portfolio. For safety, shift about 25% of your stock portfolio into high-dividend stocks, such as utilities. Maintain another 40% in intermediate-term Treasuries. The remaining 20% should be kept in cash-equivalent investments.

Consider investing in tax-exempt bond funds if your joint adjusted gross income tops $32,000. At that level, one-half of your social security benefits become taxable.

Choose payout and investment options for your IRAs, Keoghs, and employer retirement plans. Consult a tax professional about the tax consequences of making lump-sum withdrawals.

Look into long-term-care insurance early in your retirement. These policies partially defray the catastrophic cost of prolonged nursing care. The cost rises steeply once you reach your 60s, however, and may be prohibitively expensive if you wait too long.

Hire an estate tax attorney to develop an estate plan. Set up revocable living trusts to avoid probate. If your joint estate will exceed $600,000, see an attorney about setting up a bypass trust to avoid estate tax. Purchase life insurance to pay any anticipated estate taxes. Update your wills to include new trust provisions and to create testamentary trusts for your grandchildren. See Chapter 10 for a complete discussion of estate planning, including bypass trusts.

Begin a program of gift-giving to your children and grandchildren. You may make joint gifts of up to $20,000 per person each year without being subject to gift tax.

Open custodian accounts for each grandchild.

10 INVESTMENT "MUSTS"

Chasing wealth is like flying with homemade wings. You never know if you'll soar or you'll fall. Before you leap, therefore, it's best to have a safe place to land. The 10 "musts" listed below will serve as your launching pad. Build this security first, and your family finances will be invulnerable, even if your high-flying investments are made of wax.

1. Build an emergency cash reserve equal to 3 to 6 months' living expenses. Fine-tune the amount to your own circumstances by considering what misfortunes could occur that would not be covered by your health and disability insurance. Keep your emergency cache where you can get to it quickly, such as in money market mutual funds.

2. Once you have your emergency fund, begin saving at least 5% of your combined take-home pay. Because you probably won't touch these dollars for a while, this money can be invested in riskier, long-term investment vehicles with potential for higher return. Increase the amount you save by at least 1% per year until you are saving 20% of your income.

3. If your employer offers a 401(k) or salary-reduction plan, go for it. If you qualify to set up an IRA or Keogh, do so. Contribute every dollar you can. These are terrific ways to save for retirement. You don't pay tax on the amount you contribute, and your retirement fund compounds tax-deferred. The earlier you start, the better. A single $5,000 Keogh contribution at age 25 will grow twenty times as large as the same $5,000 contributed at age 60 (before withdrawal at age 70½). Even if you cannot deduct your IRA, your tax-sheltered retirement funds still grow substantially larger than they would in a taxable account.

4. Tie up no more than 20% of net income in consumer debt. Assign 10% of your income to debt repayments until you meet that goal. Pay off all credit card debt as it becomes due. If you can't stop charging, perform "plastic surgery." Discard all but one or two major bank cards, for use only in emergencies. Consider taking out a home-equity loan to pay off some of your high-interest debts if ready cash is not available. If you cannot make any progress in reducing your debt, visit a local consumer credit counseling service.

5. Diversify to minimize risk and increase profit potential. Spread your assets among investments that provide liquidity, an inflation hedge (such as a home), and a share in the nation's prosperity (such as common stock). If you are buying stock, diversify over time and over several stocks in different industries. No-load mutual funds are a practical and time-efficient way to diversify. Be sure to choose funds that have done well in both up and down market cycles. But don't get carried away. It is difficult to follow more than a dozen companies, even with lots of spare time.

6. In buying stocks, go for value. Don't buy at the top. Wait for a stock you believe is undervalued. Use dollar-cost averaging to lower your overall purchase price.

WINNING STOCK COMBINATIONS: SIZING UP STOCK VALUES ON YOUR OWN

Follow these guidelines:
Price-earnings ratio of 10 or under
Return on equity of 15% or more
Price not more than two times book value
Cash and receivables equal to or better than current
    liabilities
Low debt (not more than a third of capitalization)
Good management
Dividend of more than 8% if going for income, 4% for
    growth-income

---

7. Purchase solid health insurance coverage. If your employer's health benefits do not cover certain expenses, such as dental care or prescriptions, consider whether supplemental insurance is cost-effective. Dovetail your company benefits to make sure your family is adequately, but affordably, insured. With two plans to choose from, two-earners can minimize insurance costs. Pick the best, most affordable parts of each plan. Evaluate the amount of deductibles, percentage levels of reimbursement, the kind and length of treatments covered, the amount of any employee contributions, and the difficulty or expense of rejoining each health plan if it is dropped. If your spouse's plan provides adequate and inexpensive insurance for the whole family, for example, opt for the least comprehensive protection in your own.

8. Buy disability insurance replacing 60% to 70% of your take-home pay (after-tax income if you are self-employed), with payments beginning 90 days after you become disabled or after your accrued sick pay will run out. If you are under 65, the odds of suffering a serious disability are far greater than the odds of death. Buy supplemental policies to bridge any gap in employer-provided coverage. For top-notch protection, your contract should include: (*a*) disability defined as inability to perform the duties of your own occupation; (*b*) noncancelable clause; (*c*) partial disability payments if you go back to work for a fraction of your salary; (*d*) benefits payable to age 65 or for life; (*e*) Social Security rider providing for increased benefits if you are ineligible for social security disability income; and (*f*) cost-of-living rider guaranteeing an annual benefit increase to compensate for inflation.

9. Buy life insurance if you have children, especially if you are self-employed. As a rule of thumb, your coverage should equal at least five times your gross salary. But discuss your exact needs with an insurance agent or financial planner. Because both of you work, both of you should be insured. Before you buy, shop around. Term insurance is generally the least expensive option until you reach your late 40s or early 50s. Switch to universal or single-premium life when you reach this stage of life. Reassess your needs first, however, and reduce coverage if warranted.

10. Write a will. To make sure that your assets pass to your intended heirs without undue hardship and expense, you must have a will. In addition to spelling out your bequests, a will lets you name an executor for your estate and a guardian for your children. If you die without a will, a court will make these decisions for you according to your state law.

5

EQUAL RITES:
Law and Finance

One of my clients worries constantly that he has,
is about to, or will tumble off a legal precipice at
any second. The first two calls he makes every morning are
to his lawyer and his astrologer. I exaggerate, of course. The
point is, my client knows something that most of us tend to
forget. Law, like gravity, is often an unseen force. We don't
think about it until we walk off the cliff. Many of my clients
make financial decisions without a thought as to their possible legal consequences. Then they look down and find that,
like Wily Coyote, they're in midair.

Law and finance are as inseparable as love and marriage.
You can't borrow, take out insurance, or buy property without contracts. You can't spend or invest without bumping
into banking and securities laws. Estate planning entangles
you in trusts and wills.

This doesn't mean that you need a lawyer in your pocket.
But you do need to be aware that investing involves more
than the give-and-take of money. Remember that law plays
a part, too, and consult a lawyer before you set any major
or long-term plans in motion. This is particularly true if you

are investing in commercial and residential real estate, starting up or incorporating your own business, setting up a self-employment pension plan, considering limited partnerships or tax shelters, or planning your estate.

This chapter focuses on the law as it relates to the finances of married couples in four areas: (1) holding title to marital property; (2) protecting marital assets from creditors; (3) establishing credit in both spouses' names; and (4) pregnancy and rights in the workplace.

TAKING TITLE

Before hanging out my shingle, I was general counsel for a young California corporation. One of my duties was to issue stock certificates to new shareholders. We were brash and outrageously optimistic, with visions of nationwide offices and private jets in our heads. Our investors were hand-picked, and I knew each and every one of them.

They were oilmen, executives, doctors. Because it was a private offering, all of them had to swear that they were sophisticated investors with net worths in excess of $200,000. All of them were married. But only a handful of these savvy backers had any idea how they wanted to take title to their securities.

"Joint tenants with right of survivorship?" I would ask.

"That sounds good."

"Or community property?"

"Okay. Whatever you think best."

None of them seemed to think it mattered much. Just another lawyer muddying the water. But the way you take title, especially to real estate, can play a crucial role in tax and estate planning, in protecting marital assets from creditors, and in divorce.

How should you take title? It doesn't seem like such a tough question. Most couples would promptly say, "Joint." After all, marriage means sharing, not splitting. No argument. Joint ownership may be best for you. More than sentiment should go into your decision, however. Joint or separate, your choice should be based on the type and value of your assets, whether you may be liable to creditors, and how you want the property distributed at death.

Nor is "joint" a complete answer. Joint ownership can take several forms, and the one you choose will determine how much control you each have over the disposition and taxation of your property. And you must decide whether *all* of your assets—home, bank accounts, stocks, and other investments—will be held jointly. As we'll see, owning everything jointly can have dire estate tax consequences.

Before you decide, let's review your options. There are four types of joint ownership.

Joint Tenancy with Right of Survivorship

This is the most common way for spouses to take title. Each spouse owns a one-half interest and is entitled to one-half of any income or loss from the property. Either of you can sell or give away your one-half interest without the other's approval. This right could cause problems in a divorce if only one spouse has converted separate assets into joint tenancy. He or she could lose half of his or her assets.

You can't bequeath your share. That's because joint tenancy is like a tontine. Survivor takes all. For example, Greg and Cheryl own their home as joint tenants. At Greg's untimely death, his share in the house automatically passes to

Cheryl. This is true even if Greg set up a living trust or left a will to the contrary.

Benefits of joint tenancy. Not many authorities have a kind word for joint tenancy. Its popularity probably stems more from sentiment and custom. For example, most escrow companies and real estate offices automatically put title in joint tenancy when a couple buys a house. If you want to buck convention after reading this chapter, be sure to specify the type of ownership you want when buying real property.

Simplicity is probably its greatest appeal. Joint tenancy is easy to create, and at death property passes to the surviving spouse without the cost and delay of probate.

Some people believe an added benefit is that joint tenancy eliminates the need for a will. Not so—unless every knick-knack, trinket, and plug nickel are in joint tenancy when you die. How can you be sure you won't win the lottery just days, or hours, before keeling over? And a will is a backup if you and your spouse die at the same time.

Creating a joint tenancy is as easy as typing "joint tenants, with right of survivorship" on the deed. Joint tenancy bank accounts use the same language (sometimes abbreviated JTWROS). Your bank or title company will usually take care of this. What about property that doesn't have a document of title, such as jewelry, artwork, or furniture? Set down in writing that you and your spouse own the property "as joint tenants." There is no need to record this document.

If you want to transfer property you already own into joint tenancy, check your state law for the exact wording needed.

The right of survivorship avoids probate, not paperwork. The deceased spouse's name must be taken off the deed or other title document, or the survivor won't be able to mortgage or sell the property. This is done by filing a copy of the death certificate with the appropriate government official or recorder of title, along with a document stating that the surviving spouse is the sole owner. To end a joint tenancy in real estate, an "Affidavit of Death of Joint Tenant" can be used. You can buy this form in most office supply stores.

Drawbacks of joint tenancy. Those of you who believe in free will should steer clear of joint tenancy. It's like being handcuffed together, with each of you having only one of the keys. Once you put property, particularly real estate, in joint tenancy, it can't be sold without the approval of both joint tenants. You can sell your half, but this is often impractical. Where do you draw the chalk line when you sell half of your home? You sell the living room and kitchen? Your spouse, the bedrooms and den?

You also lose control over who inherits the property if you die first. Your share of all joint tenancy property passes to your surviving spouse. When he or she dies, the entire estate will go to his or her named beneficiaries. If you had children from a prior marriage, for instance, a wicked step-spouse could freeze them out.

The right of survivorship itself can be a pitfall. The company that your talent, training, and time created won't last a fiscal quarter if your surviving spouse has no interest in or aptitude for the business.

Finally, creditors can attach, or seize, a debtor spouse's one-half share of joint property. A court may then order the whole property sold to pay off the debt.

Tax considerations. Putting property in joint tenancy lets you split any income or loss equally if you file separate returns. This might produce a tax savings if you live in a separate property state. If you combine both of your incomes and losses on a joint return, there is no tax effect.

Joint tenancy can cost a bundle in estate taxes and income

tax to the surviving spouse, however. One culprit is "stepped up" basis.

Its intent is actually benevolent: to give the survivor the benefit of any appreciation in the value of the inherited share. But even bigger tax savings can result from holding the property separately, or in certain states as community property, as we'll see.

Basis is the value of an asset. A property's basis depends upon how it was acquired. For example, the basis of property you buy is generally its cost. If you inherit the same property, your basis is its fair market value. Basis is used to determine the taxable gain when property is sold. The difference between the sales price (less selling expenses) and your basis is income (or loss).

If Sam and Ellen buy their home as joint tenants, each spouse's basis is equal to half of the cost. For example, if the house cost $200,000, Sam's basis would be $100,000, and so would Ellen's. It does not matter how much Sam or Ellen actually contributed to purchasing the property.

Suppose now that Ellen dies. Thanks to a boom market, the home is worth $300,000 at the date of her death. Sam automatically acquires Ellen's interest in the home as the survivor. Sam's basis in his one-half interest ($100,000) does not change. However, his basis in Ellen's share is not her original basis, but its fair market value at the date of her death (or six months later, if the executor chooses).

Ellen's share has a stepped-up basis. Half of the basis has been stepped up from its original cost of $100,000 to its fair market value of $150,000. Sam's new basis after Ellen's death is, therefore, $250,000. This is a substantial benefit when the property is sold for a gain, because by increasing the basis for half the property, $50,000 ($150,000 minus $100,000) escapes tax. Forever.

What's so bad about that? Nothing. It's just that Sam

might have avoided tax on *all*, not half, of the appreciation if the property had been held differently. For example, if the house had been in Ellen's name alone, Sam's basis as her heir would be its full fair market value, $300,000. If he sells it for that price, he would have no taxable gain whatsoever. But as a joint tenant, he would be taxed on $50,000 ($300,000 minus $250,000 stepped-up basis). The income tax on $50,000 is likely to dwarf the probate fees avoided. Placing property in a living trust or community property will achieve the same result (see below).

That's all well and good if you know who's going to die first. At least with joint tenancy, half of the basis gets stepped up. Isn't that better than nothing if you guess wrongly in the game of Tenancy Roulette? In some cases, yes. Couples who buy property together using community property of fairly equal amounts of their separate funds will face the same income tax liabilities regardless of how they take title.

Joint tenancy can also cause estate tax troubles. If all of your property goes to your surviving spouse, it may push her or his estate over the amount exempt from estate tax. The result: a painful—and unnecessary—tax bill.

If you each hold some or all of your property separately, you can use such estate-planning devices as marital trusts and bequests to take full advantage of the $600,000 exemption (see Chapter 10).

Note: You do not have to worry about the estate tax consequences of joint tenancy if you are confident that your marital estate will not exceed $600,000.

Tenancy by the Entirety

Almost half the states recognize this form of ownership dating back to Magna Carta. It operates exactly like a joint tenancy, with the following exceptions:

1. Only married couples can own property as tenants by the entirety and, therefore, it ends on divorce.

2. You cannot sell or give away your share without your spouse's consent.

Because ownership is not divisible, you have more protection from creditors. If a debt is incurred by you or your spouse alone, property held as tenants by the entirety usually cannot be sold to satisfy the debt.

The tax considerations discussed above for joint tenancy apply equally to tenancy by the entirety.

Community Property

In nine states, title to everything a couple acquires after marriage is automatically held jointly as community property. The exceptions are gifts and inheritances. These community-property states are: Arizona, California, Idaho, Louisiana, Nevada, New Mexico, Texas, Washington, and Wisconsin.

Like tenancy by the entirety, community property gives both of you an equal and undivided interest in all marital assets and income. This keeps creditors at bay.

When one spouse dies, half of his or her share of the community property goes to the surviving spouse. The other half goes to the beneficiary named in the deceased spouse's will.

You can enjoy the best of both worlds by holding your community property in joint tenancy. Joint tenancy lets you avoid probate. Community property gives you an income tax advantage denied other forms of joint ownership (see below). Make sure the title document uses the phrase "community property held in joint tenancy."

Tax considerations. Sometimes on a rainy day, the sun will break through and shine on one favored spot. In much the same way, the Internal Revenue Code shines solely on community property. *Both* shares of community property held in joint tenancy receive a stepped-up basis upon the death of one spouse.

For example, suppose Jim and Rebecca bought their family home for $90,000. The home was community property held in joint tenancy. When Rebecca died, the home's fair market value had risen to $140,000. Jim's basis is stepped up to the fair market value of the entire property, or $140,000. If he were to sell the home after Rebecca's death for its fair market value, Jim would have no taxable gain.

Compare this with how Jim would fare if the home were held as joint tenants or tenants by the entirety. He would inherit Rebecca's half at its appreciated value of $70,000 ($140,000 × 50%). Jim's basis in his share would still be $45,000 ($90,000 × 50%). His stepped-up basis would thus be $115,000. Selling the house would result in a $25,000 gain ($140,000 fair market value minus $115,000 basis).

To benefit from the tax code's favoritism, you must be able to prove to the IRS that the joint tenancy property has a double identity as community property. Keep records to show that the property and any improvements were paid for with community funds.

What are the estate tax consequences of community property laws? If the first spouse to die leaves the property to the surviving spouse, the result is the same as with joint tenancy—a tax-free transfer due to the unlimited marital deduction. If the property does not pass to the surviving spouse, taxability will depend on the value of the property and the deceased spouse's taxable estate.

When the surviving spouse dies, the result is again the same as with joint tenancy. The value of the surviving spouse's estate in excess of the $600,000 exemption is fully taxed.

Tenancy in Common

If you want to own property in unequal shares, you must become tenants in common. Normally, the division is made in proportion to each person's payments for the property (for example, down payment, mortgage, taxes, and insurance). Each tenant has an equal right to use the property, however.

Each tenant can dispose of his or her share without the other's approval. Or he can bring legal action to end the tenancy in common. In that case, the property is divided or sold and the proceeds distributed in proportion to each tenant's share. The tenancy agreement usually gives each tenant the right to buy the other's share in case of divorce.

There is no right of survivorship. Your share of the property can be transferred by will. Probate cannot be avoided without using a living trust.

Tenancy in common is best for unmarried persons. Unless your goal is to create unequal shares, consider the other three types of joint ownership described above.

Tax considerations. If you inherit your spouse's share, your basis in the property is equal to your original basis plus the fair market value of your deceased spouse's interest at the date of death. Thus, if you owned 60% of the family home and your deceased spouse 40%, you would receive a stepped-up basis for 40% of the property. Compare this to joint tenancy, where each spouse holds an equal share, and 50% of the basis is stepped up.

No estate taxes are due when the first spouse dies if the property is left to the surviving spouse. When the second spouse dies, the portion of his or her estate exceeding $600,000 will be taxed. If the property does not go to the surviving spouse, it may or may not be taxed depending upon its value and the value of the decedent's estate.

$ $ $

What are the alternatives to joint ownership? You can take title separately in your or your spouse's name alone. Or you can set up trusts to deal with some of the dilemmas posed by joint ownership.

PROTECTING MARITAL ASSETS FROM CREDITORS

Debt is not always a slowly rising mound of bills. Sometimes it strikes with the suddenness of a shark, dragging you under before you can protect yourselves. Dan's furniture business was slapped with a liability suit when one of his drivers collided with a motorcyclist. Elaine and Chris were sued for personal injury damages when a house guest slipped and did a backflip into their Jacuzzi. Roy, whose duties included writing checks, was left to face the IRS when his employer skipped town without paying over $100,000 in payroll taxes.

All of these folks were honest, well educated, and prudent. All of them were broadsided by unforeseen events. That's why preserving marital assets should always be a part of your financial planning, especially if you are a small business owner subject to economic downturns, competition, and liability suits or if you are involved in speculative investments or business deals. Minimizing your risk of loss requires knowledge of your state's property laws and legal means of sheltering assets.

Whose Liability?

Responsibility for your spouse's debts depends on several factors: who incurred the debt, whether it was incurred before or during marriage, and which state you call home.

State laws regarding *premarital* debts range from total responsibility for your spouse's debts to no responsibility except for necessities. The general rule is that debts incurred before marriage remain separate debts and only the debtor spouse's separate property may be used to pay off those debts. However, when certain separate debts are incurred based on the promise of the upcoming marriage, community property or the other spouse's separate property can be levied to satisfy those debts.

In some community-property states, such as California, all community property, except a spouse's earnings after marriage, are liable for debts and personal injury damages incurred before marriage. The separate property of the non-debtor spouse is not liable.

If premarital debts are your concern, consult your lawyer for information about your particular state's law.

Whether you are responsible for your spouse's debts *during* marriage is also determined by the laws of your domicile. Generally, in separate-property states, debts of an individual spouse are separate and may be satisfied only out of separate property, unless they are secured by jointly owned property or the separate property of the other spouse.

In separate-property states, all marital assets are either "his" or "hers." But in the nine community-property states, all income and assets acquired after marriage (except by gift or inheritance) are "theirs." Generally, these community assets can be tapped by creditors of either spouse—even if only one spouse's earnings went to the purchase of an asset. Community property is normally liable for personal injury damages as well, if the spouse who committed the injury was engaged in an activity for the benefit of the family. Your separate property, however, is not liable for a spouse's debts unless he or she was acting as your agent. Even so, your separate property may be seized to pay for your spouse's necessities, if there is no community property.

Again, you should check the provisions of your state law to see if they vary from the general rule.

Legal Protections

Many states have homestead laws exempting all or part of the equity in the marital home from creditors. In some states, certain household and personal possessions are exempt as well. Texas, for example, prohibits creditors from taking the family home, automobile, furniture, clothing, and tools of your trade. In Pennsylvania, your home may not be safe, but your clothes, school books, and Bible are. Farm states protect tractors, farm equipment, and teams of horses and mules.

Restrictions on IRS seizure. Not even the dreaded IRS can take your last dime. Congress has legislated compassion by exempting certain items from IRS levy. A levy is a taking to satisfy a tax liability. There are two types of levy: levy on property that is being held for you by a third party, such as your employer or your bank, and levy on property in your possession.

If you fail to respond to a notice of levy, the IRS first raids your bank account or your salary. Your employer must turn over your paycheck to the IRS after subtracting a minimum exemption amount. You are allowed to keep a weekly amount equal to your standard deduction plus your personal exemptions divided by 52. The IRS pockets the balance.

If waylaying your bank account and garnishing your wages doesn't do the trick, the IRS looks around for other targets. Accounts receivable, promissory notes, and securities are all fair game. However, some property is excluded, including (1) clothing (except furs and jewelry) and school books; (2) food, fuel, furniture, and personal effects, up to $1,650 in value; (3) books and tools used in your profession, up to $1,100 in value; (4) income needed to pay court-ordered child support; (5) certain annuity and pension payments; (6) unemployment benefits and worker's compensation; and (7) undelivered mail.

The above items are specifically exempted by law. But as a matter of policy and public relations, the IRS rarely levies on social security benefits, Medicare or welfare payments, the cash loan value of insurance policies, death benefits, or pension plan proceeds, including IRA and Keogh accounts.

The family home is seized only as a last resort.

Taking Shelter

This is your chance to enter the world of financial intrigue—to fancy yourself as a cross between J. P. Morgan and James Bond. Secret vaults, offshore banks, Berettas that double as pocket calculators.

I have at least three clients who inhabit this fantasyland, forming Dutch corporations to take title to property or banking in the Cayman Islands. They are obsessed with ensuring that no one can ever touch—much less tax—their assets.

There are other ways to thwart creditors, however. Certainly less time-consuming ones. After all, you can't drop by the Cayman Islands to cash a check on your lunch hour.

Ownership. One simple way to protect property is to put it in someone else's name. If you own a start-up business and worry about bankruptcy, put title to cherished property, such as the family home, in your spouse's name. If you bought a commercial building in Texas before the bust and doubt that you can pay off the loan, transfer unprotected property to custodian accounts for your children (see Chapter 8 for information about custodian accounts).

Timing is important. If you wait until all is lost to change title, your creditors can set the transfer aside as in contemplation of bankruptcy.

In community-property states, all assets acquired during marriage are community property regardless of whose name is on the deed. You can, however, keep separate property in your or your spouse's name alone.

The vulnerability of jointly held assets depends upon the form of ownership. Creditors can seize one spouse's share of property that you own as joint tenants or tenants in common. That can force the sale of real estate.

On the other hand, property held as tenants by the entirety usually cannot be sold to satisfy a debt. The same is true for community property. Note that this does not protect such easily divisible assets as cash or securities. But it does protect real estate.

Irrevocable living trusts. It doesn't take a spark of the divine to create a legal person. It takes a lawyer. Such entities as trusts or corporations are persons in the eyes of the law, and as such, they may own property—your property. Transferring assets to a trust is like giving them to a friend for safekeeping. Your creditors can't force your friend (or a trust) to hand them over; he (or it) isn't liable for your debts.

There's just one catch. The trust must be irrevocable. Once title is transferred, the property isn't yours anymore. You can't take it back. Ever. What happens to it? That's up to you. You set the terms. You can set up a trust for the benefit of your spouse, your children, your friends, or a charity. The trust usually pays out any income it earns to the beneficiaries for a number of years, then ends by distributing all the property as you direct. For example, the trust can provide that your children each receive his or her share of the property when he or she reaches age 21.

The trust must be bona fide; it cannot be created solely to defraud creditors. Plan ahead. Don't wait until the crisis looms before you.

If you want to use a trust to protect assets from creditors, see your lawyer. Fees for setting up a trust range from $500 to $1,500 or more. If you name a trustee other than yourself, such as a bank, trustee fees can also be high.

For more information about trusts, see Chapter 10.

S corporations. If you want to safeguard an ongoing business, consider converting it to an S corporation. Like a trust, a corporation can take title. In this case, you transfer the assets of your business to a newly formed corporation in exchange for stock. Your creditors can take the stock, but because the shares aren't publicly traded, they have no value except to you. All they can collect are dividends—if the corporation pays any.

An S corporation is preferred over a regular ("C") corporation because it passes through its income, along with any deductions, losses, and credits, to you. The corporation doesn't pay tax—you do. This saves you the bother of putting yourself on the payroll and the expense of additional payroll tax. If the business is highly profitable, you may even save taxes by being in a lower tax bracket than the corporation.

S corporation status must be elected. To qualify, there cannot be more than 35 shareholders or more than one class of stock. The election must be filed with the IRS on or before the fifteenth day of the third month of the corporation's taxable year to be effective for that year.

There are shortcomings. Corporations are costly to set up and a nuisance to maintain. State agencies you never knew existed inundate you with a flood of demanding paperwork. Corporate tax returns must be filed. You must have a board of directors, hold annual meetings, issue stock, and take corporate minutes.

For these reasons, you may find incorporating more trouble than it's worth, unless you fear truly crippling liability or debt.

Beating the IRS

Next to the Mob, the most fearsome creditor is the IRS. And with reason. In many cases, the IRS may seize assets and ask questions later. But not even the IRS is unstoppable. Where the law has put up a protective shield, all creditors, including the IRS, are left standing on the outside looking in.

The most effective shield is transferring ownership. You can do this in two ways: Sell the property or simply put another person's name on the deed. Either action is legal—if you play by the rules.

Rule 1: A sale of property must be for full and adequate consideration. In other words, for what it is worth. Handing the deed to your home over to a relative for $1 to prevent collection of tax due may be considered a fraudulent conveyance. In that case, the IRS can go to court to have the transfer set aside or go after your relative for the value of the transferred property.

You can sell assets even if there are already outstanding

liens on the property. The IRS is not worried—federal tax liens, like leeches, usually stick with the property. Some state laws let the IRS seize property sold to another person if the lien was filed before the sale. In other states, the IRS may foreclose after filing suit.

Rule 2: A transfer of title for no or less-than-adequate consideration may still be legal. It depends on the timing. The law assumes that you know tax will be due at the time you receive taxable income. At that moment, a tax debt exists. It doesn't matter that your return has not yet been filed or the tax assessed. Transferring title without consideration once tax is owed makes the person to whom you transferred the property liable for your debt. The IRS can recover the amount of unpaid taxes from the transferee by bringing a civil suit or making an administrative assessment.

The transferee generally will not be liable if the transfer took place before the tax debt was incurred, unless a court determines that you fraudulently intended to put the property out of the reach of creditors.

Separate returns. If you will owe more taxes than you believe you will ever be able to pay, you should consider filing a separate, rather than a joint, return. This limits the IRS collection efforts to assets owned in your name alone or as a joint tenant. Assets owned jointly as tenants by the entirety or as community property cannot be seized to satisfy the tax due on a separate return. Nor can assets held in your spouse's name.

If you are unsure whether filing separately is advisable, consult your tax preparer.

For information about liability on a joint return, see Chapter 7.

Form of doing business. The major advantage of incorporation is limited liability. Property owned by the corporation cannot be seized by the IRS to pay your debts. The corporation is a separate taxpayer. Not so, sole proprietorships and partnerships. These forms of doing business expose your personal assets to possible attachment from creditors, including the IRS.

If you are in business for yourself or plan to go into business, seek legal advice about what form of doing business is best for you.

ESTABLISHING CREDIT

As a two-earner couple, you probably consider yourselves good credit risks. You don't expect to be discriminated against because you are married. After all, being married and bringing in two incomes is the reason you have an above-average family income. But until recently, creditors could judge a married couple's creditworthiness by using tests that were both stupid and cruel.

I remember a telephone conversation between our bookkeeper, Ingrid, and a mortgage lender. She and her husband were a two-earner couple, and the lender was alarmed that Ingrid might become pregnant. Apparently, the fate of the entire mortgage hinged on this one point. Our desks were side by side; I couldn't help overhearing. Appalled and embarrassed, I listened as she was gradually forced into the humiliating admission that she was barren—and her promise to submit a doctor's statement that she could never have children.

That was less than 20 years ago. Today, thanks to the

Equal Credit Opportunity Act, you and your spouse cannot be discriminated against based on sex or marital status. Instead, creditors must rely on more rational tests, such as income, length of employment, indebtedness, and credit history.

No law will end discrimination overnight, however. You must know your rights and assert them. The Equal Credit Opportunity Act provides the following protections:

Child-bearing Plans

Creditors can no longer ask whether you plan to have children or what kind of birth control practices either of you uses. Nor can they assume anything about your intentions.

Income

At your request, creditors must consider both spouses' full- and part-time income. One spouse's income may not be discounted. For example, a creditor may not count 100% of a husband's income, but only 50% of the wife's, in deciding whether a couple qualifies for a mortgage.

A creditor may, however, consider whether income is steady and reliable—for example, where the source is alimony or part-time wages.

Separate Accounts

If either of you applies for an individual account in your own name, relying on your own income, a creditor may not ask for any information about your spouse's income or credit history. The only exception is for residents of community-property states, whose earnings are never legally one spouse's alone. If you are creditworthy, a creditor may not require that your spouse be a cosigner.

Of course, both of your signatures are required if you apply together for a joint account or if you rely on jointly owned property to prove that you are a good credit risk. Where a mortgage or other loan is secured by property, a creditor may require the signature of the person who holds an interest in the property.

Your Own Name

You have the right to open a credit account under the name you use, whether it is your given name, your spouse's surname, or a combination of the two (for example, Ann Clancy, Ann Hayden, or Ann Clancy-Hayden). Using a courtesy title (Ms., Mrs., or Mr.) is optional.

If a woman changes her name upon marriage, she need only notify creditors of the name change. She cannot be required to reapply to keep the account, convert the account into a joint account with her husband, or change the account to her husband's name.

Credit Histories

If both husband and wife agree to pay the bills on a joint account or if both are allowed to use an individual account, a creditor must report credit information in both spouses' names.

Reasons for Denial

Denied credit? A creditor must spell out the specific reasons or supply an address where you can write to find out.

Enforcing Your Rights

If you suspect discrimination, cite the law to the creditor, and ask for reconsideration. If you are still dissatisfied, write to your state consumer protection agency or banking commission. Also write to the federal agency that has jurisdiction over the creditor or to the Bureau of Consumer Protection, Federal Trade Commission, Washington, DC 20560.

You may also sue in federal court for actual damages, plus up to $10,000 in punitive damages. If you win, the court will award you court costs, plus a reasonable amount for attorney's fees.

PREGNANCY AND RIGHTS IN THE WORKPLACE

Ask your employer how he feels about motherhood and apple pie, and there will be tears in his eyes as he hums the National Anthem. Ask how he feels about motherhood and working women, and he is likely to sing a different tune.

Childbearing may be exalted in our society, but it is begrudged in the workplace. Historically, U.S. employers were free to set arbitrary rules regarding pregnant workers—when they had to leave, how long they had to stay away, whether they could return at all. Simon Legrees turned suddenly paternalistic when employees became pregnant. They had to be "protected" for their own good—even if it cost them their benefits, seniority, and jobs.

The 1978 Pregnancy Discrimination Act finally and firmly rejected this Victorian logic. An employer can no longer refuse to hire you because you are pregnant—even if your due date is next week. Pregnant women who are able to work must be treated like other healthy workers. Whether you are physically able to work is a matter for you and your doctor to determine.

Pregnancy must be treated like any other medical condition. If you are pregnant and cannot work, you do not have to be kept on the job, any more than a man with a broken arm does. But even if you are unable to do part of your job (or if the fetus might be harmed by your continuing in that job), you have the right to transfer to another job if other workers with health problems have the same right.

The law also requires that a woman disabled by pregnancy be granted the same sick-leave pay, the same health insurance, and the same amount of time off as a disabled man. Pregnant women still capable of working are not entitled to sick-leave benefits. Some women may be able to work up to the moment of labor; others may be disabled by complications early in their pregnancies.

Many employers still offer limited, if any, sickness and disability benefits. Some exempt childbirth from health insurance plans. Others require women to pay a higher deductible for pregnancy than for other disabilities. These schemes are illegal.

You are entitled to an extension of sick leave if it is granted to employees with other disabilities. You are also probably entitled to voluntary time off for child-rearing and family emergencies if your employer grants other employees leave for non-job-related purposes.

Any policy regulating pregnant women—when maternity leave must begin and how long it lasts, what happens to seniority and other benefits, and the circumstances of reinstatement—must apply equally to other workers who are temporarily disabled.

The federal law is lacking in one area. It fails to set any national policy regarding parental or maternity leave benefits. The United States lags far behind other industrialized nations in this regard. In Sweden, for example, women receive 38 weeks of paid leave and 90% of their normal pay after childbirth. The number of paid weeks is 22 in Italy, 14 to 19 weeks in West Germany, 26 weeks in France, 15 weeks in Canada, and 12 weeks in Japan. The percent of pay received varies from 60% in Japan to 95% in West Germany.

Some states do afford benefits under their labor laws. In Massachusetts, for example, certain pregnant workers are guaranteed an eight-week unpaid maternity leave and no loss of seniority or accrued benefits. In California, you can request up to four months of maternity leave if you are disabled because of the pregnancy or childbirth. You are entitled to up to six weeks' disability for a normal pregnancy. To find out your rights, contact the agency that enforces your state's antidiscrimination laws.

If you believe your employer has discriminated against you because of your pregnancy, you should file a complaint with the federal Equal Employment Opportunity Commission (if your workplace has at least fifteen employees) or with your state's antidiscrimination agency. If you are a union member, your union's grievance procedure may provide a remedy.

6

PYRAMID POWER: Wealth-Building Through Real Estate

At the height of the New Gold Rush, carloads of home buyers circled *For Sale* signs like sharks within hours after properties were listed. During those glory days, a client couple of mine left the sales office to view a model home, only to return minutes later and be told the price had gone up $9,000. In 1988, home prices jumped a dizzying 30% in California.

The inflationary spree was not confined to California, either. Real estate was the black gold of the eighties. Couples who jumped aboard early became the envy of Arab emirates. A large number of them became "equity émigrés"—couples who cashed in their windfalls and bid farewell to the rat race.

But for many Americans, buying that first home was like trying to board a runaway train. They couldn't save money as fast as homes were appreciating. By the time they scraped together 20% of the purchase price, they discovered the train had already barreled past.

Well, at long last, the train is running out of steam. Home prices are leveling off or even declining across the nation. Suddenly it's a buyers' market. For two-earner couples suffering from "home sickness"—that agonized feeling they will be renters all their lives—this is good news indeed.

The fact is, the current price softness has made real estate even more attractive as an investment. Today is an excellent time to buy because there are more homes for sale than there are qualified buyers. And although economists predict appreciation will slow to a mere 6% to 9% a year during the 1990s, for investors willing to hold properties for up to five years, real estate remains a superior investment. Acquiring real estate, therefore, should be the keystone of any wealth-building plan.

Real estate investments come in every size and form— from shopping malls and trailer parks to mortgages and limited partnerships. Some of these are breathtaking high-wire acts with investors balanced on a tightrope of debt. But fortunes can be made in less daredevil fashion. The goal of this chapter is to help you build a solid foundation in real estate by acquiring at least three properties: (1) a home, (2) a vacation home, and (3) a residential rental property. If you meet this objective, you should be financially secure for life. Then, if you want to build empires that inspire legends, you have my blessing.

IN PRAISE OF REAL ESTATE

The fireworks that sent home prices shooting up like Roman candles in the 1980s obscured real estate's less flamboyant virtues. But with the fireworks over, it's time to examine the steady qualities that make real estate a sound investment even in more moderate times.

- **Inflation hedge.** You can do without gold, van Goghs, and shares in IBM, but you can't do without shelter. The value of real estate rises in inflationary times, mainly because it is more than an investment—we all need a place to live.
- **Appreciation potential.** Well-located real estate has historically increased in value, although not necessarily overnight, as recent headlines suggest. But long-term growth is assured, even if you're buying in a lagging market. After all, land is finite. Population is not. The law of supply and demand is at work here, and you can be the winner.
- **Safety.** No investment is risk-proof. Real estate has its ups and downs, but price declines are generally temporary. In periods of inflation, real estate is even superior to cash. Furthermore, it is insurable against most risks.
- **Leverage.** Leverage lets you enter a high-stakes game with nothing more than small change. You play with borrowed money, in some cases earning profits (and claiming tax deductions) greater than the cash you personally invested.

  With real estate, your lever is a mortgage. Your goal should be to buy property with the least money down— ideally, no more than 20% of the purchase price. If you put $20,000 down on a $100,000 home and finance the rest, you will double your money if the market value goes up to $120,000. That's without counting the tax benefits of the mortgage interest deduction. If you paid all cash, your yield would have been only 20% ($20,000 divided by $100,000).

  Why tie up $100,000 in one building anyway? With leverage, the same $100,000 could put you into

$500,000 worth of properties. If these properties increased in value by 6% a year, you could sell them in four years for a profit of $120,000. Your gain on one building would be only $24,000.

Before you begin grabbing up properties, however, remember that 1 million dollars' worth of leveraged properties are usually saddled with at least $800,000 in debt. That's a mortgage payment the size of King Kong. Go slow. Don't take on more debt than you can handle safely. Once you own a few income-producing properties, you'll be able to build faster.

The ultimate use of leverage is, of course, no-money down. "Never invest a cent of your own," trumpets one real estate guru. I have friends who slaved hundreds of hours and drove thousands of miles without finding a single seller naive or desperate enough to hand over his deed without the reassuring rustle of cash. Maybe they were unlucky. Maybe you can make a fortune in real estate starting with nothing. But I do know this: It will be a full-time job. And the time you waste tracking down a willing seller could be spent earning enough to make the down payment.

- **Collateral.** Once you have your first property, the second should be a breeze. Why? Because the equity in the first property is a terrific source of collateral. By refinancing or taking out a second mortgage or equity loan, you can come up with the down payment for another property. And another and another.
- **Tax savings.** How would you like the government as a silent partner? To put up almost a third of the cash and not ask for any security? Just buy real estate. No other sound investment provides such a wealth of tax benefits. And each tax dollar saved is like a government subsidy.

As a homeowner, you can deduct mortgage interest and property taxes. Special tax breaks are also available for second homes used as vacation rentals. And tax-shelter privileges let you sell house after house without tax on the gain.

All income-producing property, except land, can be depreciated. Depreciation is that most prized and elusive of tax benefits, a paper loss. Depreciation lets you write off the entire cost of a building over a number of years on the theory that it is losing value from wear and tear and will eventually need replacing. In fact, your property's market value is actually increasing, and in all likelihood, the building will still be standing when fax machines are in museums.

With certain limitations, you may also deduct all of your rental's operating expenses as well. This will shelter all, or most, of your taxable rental income. Any excess loss will reduce other taxable income.

- **Time savings.** Rental property requires less management than any other business. In fact, many rental owners hire management companies to cope with all but decision making.
- **Control.** Buy stock, silver, or soybeans, and all you can do is watch the tote board. Your fortune depends on takeovers, timing, and typhoons. Not so with real estate. Luck plays little part in your profit and loss. You can inspect a property and analyze its profitability before you buy. Your intelligence and energy are more valuable than your capital.

YOUR FIRST PRIORITY

Your assignment, you'll remember, is to acquire at least three properties: two homes and one rental. If you don't yet own even one, this mission may seem impossible. But thousands of Americans are buying homes each day, even though, statistically, they can't afford to. With two incomes to draw upon, you should be assured of finding real estate within your means.

Make purchasing property your first priority. If you are already an owner, now is the time to add to your holdings. Because with real estate, each property is truly a stepping-stone. Your equity in one property can be used to finance the next, and so on, until you are among the landed gentry.

Perhaps you are waiting for prices to tumble. This waiting game has never paid off. Price rises may slow, but the bottom won't fall out. Meanwhile, your income is losing to inflation, and real estate is only becoming more costly.

Don't hesitate. Buy something—anything—now. Stretch every dollar, put off the Bahamas. Beg, borrow, and budget to raise a down payment.

Then compromise. My ideal house stands on a sandstone cliff in Arizona, with ceiling-high windows giving a 180-degree view of Oak Creek Canyon. Where I actually live is another matter.

Your starter home should be a good *investment,* structurally sound and located in a thriving neighborhood with good schools, public services, and transportation. Don't worry about peeling paint and crabgrass. It doesn't have to be perfect. It only has to be yours. There are lots of right choices. The only mistake you can make is failing to choose.

Decide roughly how much you want to or can afford to

spend. Generally, the price should not exceed two and a half times your annual gross income. Your total payments for mortgage, homeowners insurance, and property taxes (city, county, and school taxes) should be no more than 28% of your gross income. One way to ensure that you don't waste time looking at properties beyond your reach is to ask a lender or realtor to prequalify you for a loan. You will be given a document stating how large a loan you can obtain. It doesn't cost anything, and it will give you an edge over other buyers, who haven't proven they can get a loan.

Now that you know your limit, stick to it. If need be, settle for less: a longer commute, a fixer-upper, a smaller yard. Or reverse your priorities. Buy your rental property first.

That's how I got my start in real estate. I was working for the government, and only the sorriest homes in California were within my grasp. For half the cost, I bought a charming place in Arizona instead. I rented it out for three years, sold it for almost double the modest purchase price, and invested the proceeds in other properties.

Beginning as a landlord gives you freedom to acquire property where your money buys the most value, even if that is out of town or out of state. It also lets you consider lower-cost condominiums and town houses, which are not good home investments. Moreover, once you come up with the down payment, a rental costs far less out-of-pocket than a home. If the property is reasonably priced, the rental income should cover all or most of your monthly payments. In effect, your tenant buys the property for you. Add to that the tax benefits, and a rental makes more economic sense than a home.

Because rental property requires some management, it's best not to purchase property more than a day's drive away. If it's in a locale you frequently visit or where you have relatives, so much the better. If you do range far afield, you can hire a management company to oversee the property. This will add to your cost, however.

A HOME OF YOUR OWN

Home ownership has the force of a biological drive for most Americans. From ocean to ocean, we are compelled to stake out our own piece of ground, erect our white picket fences, and fire up our Sunday barbecues. A home of our own is a symbol—of sanctuary, success, and democratic values. It is rarely thought of in dispassionate economic terms, as an investment.

I'm asking you to do just that. Surveys show that once our name is on the mailbox, most of us are content to cocoon and remodel. Only lack of space or a job transfer induces us to move again.

You might as well board up a gold mine. Your home is the only asset that lets you *pyramid* your way to wealth. By tapping the rich vein of equity that runs through your property, you can trade up time after time—without paying a penny in tax. Or you can use your equity to acquire income-producing real estate.

Don't buy for the ages. Buy to resell. Don't plan how long to keep your house, but how soon to get rid of it. Don't become emotionally involved. The bronzed baby shoes will fit on other mantels. Until you meet your financial goals, treat your home strictly as an investment.

I know that's asking a lot. The husband of one of my client couples has pursued this strategy for years, gradually pyramiding a $30,000 bungalow into an $800,000 mansion. They move so often their own daughter couldn't remember where to find them and went to the wrong house for the wife's birthday party one year. The husband has no more feeling for each house than he does for his bank account, but his wife needs emotional roots and is bitterly unhappy.

If being periodically uprooted will make either of you miserable, skip to the next section. There are other ways of accumulating wealth, although not in such leaps and bounds. What we're going to discuss here is a plan for using your home as the springboard for amassing a considerable fortune. The formula is simple:

1. Buy a second home and rent out the first.

2. Trade up from your second home at least twice.

3. Use the built-up equity in your last trade-up home to buy a vacation home.

The Scenario

You buy your first home with an eye for its potential as a rental property (see "Buying to Rent" on page 133). As you advance in your careers, your incomes grow. So does the value of your home. When the time is right, you take out an equity loan, with your increased equity as collateral. Using the loan proceeds as a down payment, you buy a new home, this time with an eye to reselling. You move into the second home and rent out the first. The rental income takes care of the payments on the first home.

Now you have the satisfaction of watching both properties appreciate. You sell the second house and trade up to a more expensive property, still keeping the first house rented. You trade up at least once more, then tap the equity buildup in either property to buy a vacation home.

Buying to Resell

What factors boost your odds of realizing the maximum gain when you trade up in three to seven years? First, look for neighborhoods that are in demand because they have the best public schools and the best proximity to shopping, cultural centers, and the central employment area, with the least exposure to congestion, crime, and the other sensations of urban life. Or if the choicest neighborhoods are too pricey, explore up-and-coming areas that stand to benefit from economic or physical change, such as the arrival of a new employer or a zoning change.

Choose an architectural style that conforms to the taste of the area. Cape Cod in New England, ranch in the West. Avoid such exotic or unpopular styles as Black Forest, Moorish, and 21st century at all costs.

As you trade up into higher price ranges, the largest pool of purchasers will be baby boomers who are also moving up. Make sure the house suits their needs and tastes. That means more luxury and space. The median single-family home built in 1987 was a record 1,760 square feet. Four to five bedrooms are favored. Nearly three-quarters of all homes built that year featured central air-conditioning, up from 43% in 1972. Thirty-eight percent had two bathrooms and fully one-third offered a whirlpool bath. Sixty-two percent of new homes have one or more fireplaces, compared with 38% in 1972. In fact, fireplaces add more to the resale value than any other feature in all markets.

Avoid swimming pools in all but the southern and southwestern markets. They are considered a liability when you try to resell.

Once you zero in on a likely property, hire a professional inspector to check for structural soundness. The fee—between $200 and $300—is well worth it. One of the most expensive mistakes you can make is to buy a house with more defects than you realized. Major flaws include a rotting foundation, faulty wiring, corroded pipes, and termite damage.

Co-ops, condominiums, and town houses. These forms of shared ownership offer a cheaper way for buyers to get a start in real estate. There is no reason why the first home you intend to convert to a rental should not be a co-op, condominium, or town house. For several reasons, they are poor resale investments, however.

Generally, co-op owners may not sell without the approval of the board of directors. At worst, you may never find a buyer that the board will accept if the building has strict standards. Seeking approval can also delay the sale and cost time and money in buying your new home.

You have no control over repairs and maintenance of common areas. If the building exterior and recreational facilities are allowed to deteriorate, the resale value of your unit will plummet.

An old apartment building that has been converted may have hidden structural defects, rusty plumbing, or air-conditioning that blows cold only in winter.

Finally, co-ops, condominiums, and town houses appreciate more slowly than detached homes. This means less equity to draw on when you trade up. Your move up will be much smaller.

Financing to resell. When you shop for a mortgage, remember that you will be selling in three to seven years. Don't worry about the total interest cost—you won't be paying it anyway. Concentrate on obtaining the largest loan you can comfortably afford for the smallest down payment (10% if possible). This will allow you to buy the most expensive home for your money.

The ideal mortgage, therefore, requires the lowest monthly payments. A 30-year, adjustable-rate mortgage (ARM) fits the bill. The interest rate for an ARM is usually one to three percentage points lower than that of a fixed-rate loan. The difference is substantial. For example, the monthly payment on a 30-year, $150,000 *fixed-rate loan* at 10½% is $1,372, whereas the payment on an *adjustable-rate loan* at 9% is $1,101. For $1,372 per month, you could borrow $187,000 with an ARM.

Similarly, the monthly payment on a *15-year, $150,000* adjustable-rate loan at 9% is $1,433. You can borrow $195,000 for the same monthly payment if you go for a 30-year mortgage.

A major advantage of adjustable-rate mortgages is that they are usually assumable. Because assumable loans make it easier for buyers to qualify, this enhances the salability of your home.

Don't worry that your ARM's interest rate may skyrocket. It's unlikely that rates will escalate so steeply during the short time before you sell that you would pay a higher average annual rate than you would by taking out a fixed-rate loan. Moreover, interest rates may fall, and you might enjoy even lower monthly payments. *Note:* Avoid an ARM that doesn't reduce its rate when other rates go down.

There is no benefit to prepaying the principal on your loan when you are planning to sell. You won't lower your monthly payments, and you will reduce the biggest tax advantage of home ownership—the mortgage interest deduction.

How much mortgage can you afford? As much as you are willing to devote to home ownership. Today's home buyers generally spend between 30% and 35% of their incomes for homes of their own, compared to 23% in 1965. Lenders feel that no more than 28% of your gross income should go for mortgage payments (including taxes and insurance) and that payments for *all* debt should not exceed 36%.

Don't forget settlement costs, which can range from 3% to 6% of your purchase price. These must be paid in addition to the down payment. Most costly are "points" or loan origination fees. This one-time charge is a premium you must pay up front to obtain a loan when the trend of interest rates is up. One point is equal to 1% of the loan amount. For example, if you are charged 2½ points for a $100,000 mortgage, you will pay $2,500 ($100,000 × 2.5%). Other settlement costs include title insurance, appraisals, credit reports, and escrow and recording fees.

Deduction for home mortgage interest. In many cases, the mortgage interest deduction is all that makes home buying possible these days. How many of us would cross swords with $10,000 or more a year in mortgage interest if up to 31% of it, depending on your tax bracket, were not government-subsidized? What broker would quote the monthly payment without hastening to add, "Before taxes"?

You can take shelter from taxes under more than one roof. Mortgage interest paid to acquire, construct, or substantially improve your first or second home is fully deductible as long as your total debt doesn't exceed $1 million.

The mortgage must be *secured* by the property itself. For example, if you mortgage your beach house in the Hamptons to pay for your suburban colonial, none of the interest will be deductible. The mortgage must also be obtained within 90 days before or after your purchase.

What if you are building a home? All of your interest will be deductible if you (1) finance construction from the beginning; (2) complete the project within two years; and

(3) obtain a permanent mortgage within 90 days of completion.

Suppose you build first, then finance? Mortgage interest attributable to the last 24 months of construction costs is deductible.

Once your original acquisition debt is paid off, you must deduct any new mortgage interest as home equity debt, with its $100,000 limitation (see "Home-equity debt," page 131).

What about "points" paid to obtain the loan? Generally, only "points" charged on a loan to buy or improve your principal residence are fully deductible in the year paid. All other "points"—on refinancing or your second home—must be amortized and deducted over the life of the loan. "Points" paid on an FHA or VA loan are usually a fee for services and cannot be claimed as an interest deduction.

Trading Up

Of the more than four million homes sold in 1986, roughly two-thirds went to repeat buyers, most of whom were capitalizing on the equity in their old houses to move up to more palatial digs. Because of demand, trade-up homes are expected to appreciate faster than starter homes in the 1990s.

Trading up is a stairway to riches. Say you bought a starter house five years ago for $80,000, with a $72,000 mortgage. If home prices rose 7% a year, you could sell today for $108,000. If the buyers put $20,000 down, you would walk away with roughly $48,000 in cash after paying off your mortgage and selling expenses. That will buy you a $240,000 home if you put 20% down. Repeat this process every five years, and by the time you retire (and want to trade down), you could be lords of a manor worth over $3 million.

Timing your trade. You can't set sail before casting off. Not without taking a piece of the dock. The same thing goes for trading up. If you embark on the purchase of a new home before you cast off the old, you could sink under the weight of two mortgages.

Timing is, therefore, crucial. You want the sale of your present house to coincide as closely as possible with the purchase of your next one. How you approach this tricky task depends on whether your real estate market is hopping or moribund. For example, in an area where appreciation is rampant and houses are moving within 45 days of being listed, you can be aggressive: buying your trade-up house before putting your current one on the market.

Buy in January when prices are lowest, and try for a June close. Then list your present home in March or April, and hope to close the sale in June also. This gives you a couple of extra months of appreciation on your sale. Even in an active market, however, your best-laid plans may go awry. For this reason, you should follow the aggressive approach only if you can temporarily afford two mortgage payments.

Naturally, if you live in a depressed market, you must be far less daring. Don't launch into the purchase of a new house until you cut yourselves loose from the old. If you run across a house you simply can't pass up, ask the seller to agree to a clause in the contract making the purchase contingent on the sale of your present house. The contract will expire if you can't find a buyer for your house within a specified period—usually 60 to 90 days. The seller, for his part, may ask for a contingency release clause. This gives him the right to continue to show the house. If he receives a bona fide offer, you usually have up to 72 hours to buy the house at the price you offered or release him from the contract.

How can you swing the down payment on a second home

when you are still anchored to the first? By using a swing, or bridge, loan. This type of loan lets you borrow against your equity until the first home sells. Generally, you make interest-only payments until the entire principal balance comes due, usually within 30 to 120 days.

The pyramid power of tax deferral. What do you have that every tax shelter investor madly pursues? The power to defer gain. Deferral is what tax shelters are all about. Deferral puts off the day of tax reckoning until you are in a lower bracket or have future losses or deductions.

Deferral has been scarcer than good service since tax reform. You can't buy it any more by sinking your money into Broadway shows or jojoba farms. It isn't found in the Channel Islands or Liechtenstein either. It's much closer to home. In fact, it is your home.

You can sell your present house, reap a windfall profit, and defer all tax on the gain if certain conditions are met. You can pyramid your profits time and time again. By allowing your gains to compound untaxed, buying and selling homes can produce a dramatic increase in wealth.

What are the rules? You may defer the entire gain on the sale or exchange of your home if

1. both your old and new homes were your principal residence;
2. you buy or build your new home within two years before or after the sale; and
3. your new home costs at least as much as the adjusted sales price of your old home.

If you meet these tests, the tax is postponed, not excused. The gain not taxed is subtracted from the cost of your new home, giving you a lower basis. For example, Mel and Helen sell their Mediterranean-style home for a $45,000 profit. They reinvest in a $387,000 Spanish villa one month later. Mel and Helen will not be taxed on their $45,000 gain in the year of sale. Instead, they will subtract the deferred gain from the purchase price of the villa, giving them a basis in their new home of $342,000 ($387,000 − $45,000). This is the amount they will use to compute their gain if the villa is sold.

Eventually, you may buy a lower-priced home or move into an apartment. At that time, the gain will be taxed. But even then, if you are age 55 or older, you can shelter $125,000 of your gain.

Don't get carried away, however. You can use this deferral only once every two years, unless your move is work-related.

If you do not buy a costlier home, all or part of your profit will be taxed (unless you are age 55 or older).

Principal residence. Both the old and new homes must be your principal residence. For example, a beach house where you spend the summer would not qualify.

A principal home may be a mobile home, trailer, motor home, houseboat, condominium, or stock you own in a co-operative apartment. It can also be the unit of an apartment building where you live if you are the owner.

You should be living in the home at the time of sale. If you sell your old home before you buy the new and move into temporary quarters, your old home may lose its status as your principal residence.

Time for replacement. Your replacement home must be purchased and occupied within a 48-month period—two years before or two years after you sell your old home. There is no grace period.

The replacement period is suspended for members of the armed forces and overseas employees.

Cost of your new home. If the cost of your new home is

equal to or exceeds the adjusted sales price of your old home, all of your gain is postponed. The adjusted sales price is the sales price minus selling and fixing-up expenses. Selling expenses include the broker's commission, title insurance, escrow fees, and recording fees.

Fixing-up expenses are repair costs incurred for work performed in the 90 days before the sale and paid for no later than 30 days after the sale.

If you do not buy a more expensive home, the difference between the adjusted sales price and the cost of your new home is taxed—up to the amount of the gain.

Allocation of gain between married couples. If title to your new home is held differently than title to your old residence, an allocation of the postponed gain may be necessary. For example, Ron's and Shelby's old home was Ron's separate property, but the new one is owned by both of them as joint tenants. When this happens, you and your spouse must file a consent using Form 2119, *Sale or Exchange of Principal Residence,* to postpone the gain.

The consent has the effect of dividing the adjustment to the basis of the new home equally between you and your spouse. For the consent to be effective, you both must use the old and new homes as your principal residence.

If both you and your spouse owned your own homes before marriage and sold them to buy a new one after you tied the knot, you both may defer the gains on your separate homes as long as the new home costs more than the *combined* adjusted sales prices of the old homes and you take title jointly. No consent is needed.

Reporting requirements. You must report the sale of your home even if the tax is postponed on all of the gain. Use Form 2119, *Sale or Exchange of Principal Residence,* to report the details of the sale.

If you have not yet purchased your new residence by the

filing date, you do not have to pay tax on the gain. Form 2119 must still be attached to the return, however. If some or all of the gain later proves to be taxable, you must amend your return for the year of the sale.

YOUR VACATION, OR SECOND, HOME

Why shouldn't your life be like a Club Med ad? People do live in Maui, Miami, and Malibu after all. Now that you have a stately home, why not invest for fun? A vacation home where you can play, while your money works hard.

Why a vacation home? You want more than one piece of real estate, and a vacation, or second, home (1) offers tax benefits, (2) can be rented out, and (3) is safer and in many cases easier to manage than such other real estate investments as commercial rentals, REITs, and limited partnerships. Besides, what sounds more enviably prosperous than "my ski lodge" or "my country place"?

Let your friends think it's a luxury, but buy it as an investment. Research the market thoroughly, keeping in mind that with second homes, location is paramount. Close to nature preferably—near the ocean, mountains, or lakes. A tantalizing view helps, too. Buy the best property you can afford. The better homes find buyers despite high interest rates and adverse tax laws.

Don't ignore your heart, though. Profit and pleasure should converge, even if you plan to rent the property occasionally. Choose a spot within a few hours' drive of your primary home. Nothing dampens the joy of a weekend away from home more than eight hours of traffic and backseat squabbling each way. Moreover, a second home fairly close to an urban area is easier to sell or rent.

You don't want to spend your entire weekend hammering and mowing, either. Because they need little maintenance, condominiums make good second homes.

No matter how idyllic or scenic the locale, don't expect rental income to completely cover the mortgage payments and maintenance. Vacation rentals are seasonal, and most post negative cash flows unless the down payment exceeds 20%.

Equity Financing

Your primary residence is a reservoir of equity waiting to be tapped. Why not use this resource to fund the down payment on your second home? There are three ways to draw money out of this home bank account: securing a second mortgage, refinancing your original mortgage, or establishing a home-equity line of credit. Interest on any of these forms of borrowing is equally deductible, up to a loan of $100,000.

Your best bet for a down payment is probably a **second mortgage.** You can borrow up to 80% of the market value of your first house minus the unpaid balance on your first mortgage. You have anywhere from 12 to 30 years to repay. Interest on a second mortgage is usually a percentage point or two higher than for a first mortgage. Closing costs are high, too—up to $750 in settlement fees and 3 points for obtaining the loan.

Refinancing is a way of reducing your mortgage payments when interest rates have fallen significantly. It is less desirable merely for borrowing because closing costs are considerably higher than those charged for second mortgages— from 3% to 6% of your mortgage. Furthermore, these costs are not fully deductible in the year paid. Unless the interest is at least three points lower than your current rate, refinancing will not pay.

Home-equity lines of credit are flexible, handy, and as touchy as nitroglycerin. Like a second mortgage, a home-equity loan lets you borrow from 70% to 80% of your primary home's market value minus the unpaid balance of your mortgage. You borrow by writing a check for the amount of cash you want to pull out of your house. The interest rate fluctuates monthly and is usually several percentage points above prime. Repayment is rather swift—in 5 to 10 years.

Home-equity loans are less costly than second mortgages because of lower closing costs. Count on paying about $1,500 in loan-origination fees, however.

Using a home-equity line of credit is like wielding a credit card. And as with most credit cards, only a minimum monthly payment, usually covering interest only, is required. Spot the danger? The principal, in the shape of a balloon payment the size of the *Hindenberg,* will one day come due. If you can't meet the payment, you can lose your house. Shy away from home-equity lines of credit, therefore, unless you have the discipline of Silas Marner.

Home-equity debt. You may deduct interest on up to $100,000 of home-equity debt, such as a second mortgage or home-equity line of credit. Interest paid on a refinanced loan is also subject to the $100,000 cap if the new principal amount exceeds the unpaid balance of the old mortgage.

The tax law does not set building standards. Almost any kind of dwelling can be your "home." So long as there are cooking, sleeping, and toilet facilities, your castle can be a house, time-share unit, mobile home, boat, or recreational vehicle.

A second home does not actually have to be used during the year if it is not rented to others.

"Points" paid to refinance. If you tap the equity in your first home to help buy the second, you will most likely pay "points," or loan-origination fees. These must be deducted over the life of your new mortgage.

For example, George and Betty paid $1,800 in points when they refinanced their home for cash to make the down payment on a sunny, seaside cottage. The new mortgage is for 15 years. They may deduct $10 for each monthly payment ($1,800 divided by 180 months).

Tax rules for rented vacation homes. *Any* dwelling you rent out and also use as a residence is a "vacation home" in the eyes of the tax law. As such, it is subject to special tax rules. This is true whether the property is located in the Poconos or Death Valley.

These rules set up three categories of vacation homes based upon personal versus rental use. I wish I could say that Congress's intent was pure, but the purpose of these classifications is to keep you from claiming rental losses.

The first class includes homes rented for less than 15 days. The good news is that both mortgage interest and property taxes are fully deductible. Any rental expenses are not. As consolation, your rental income is tax-free.

Most vacation home owners fall into the second category. Here the property is personally used for more than 14 days or 10% of the time it is rented, whichever is greater. Your rental expenses are now deductible, but only up to the amount of your rental income. In other words, no rental loss is allowed. The house is considered to be primarily your residence and only incidentally a rental. Because you have used the home, you must allocate your expenses between rental and personal use. (The exception is for advertising and rental commissions, which are 100% deductible.) You must deduct interest and taxes first. Any interest or taxes in excess of rental income may be claimed as an itemized deduction. If there is any rental income remaining, you may then deduct operating expenses and, lastly, depreciation. Of course, if your rental income exceeds expenses, your net profit is taxable.

If you use your home for less than 14 days a year or 10% of the time it is rented, the property is treated as a true rental. In this third category, all operating expenses allocated to rental use, plus depreciation, are deductible. Note, however, that your mortgage interest must be allocated between personal and rental use. Because the house is considered rental property, it no longer qualifies as a second home, and the personal portion of the interest is no longer deductible. The interest allocated to rental use is added to your other rental expenses.

For purposes of the vacation home rules, "personal use" means use by you, your spouse, members of your family, or anyone who pays less than fair rental value. Personal use does not include a period during which the house is your principal residence. Nor does it include days spent cleaning, maintaining, or furnishing the property.

For information about computing and reporting rental income and expenses, see "Tax Aspects of Rental Real Estate," page 141.

BUYING TO RENT

I'm not going to tell you how to make a million dollars in real estate in three years. You'll go $900,000 into debt doing it. I'm not going to tell you how to buy property for no-money down. The lone innocent still willing to swap a deed for a promise has more investors swarming around him than frangipani has bees. What I am going to tell you is how to get rich gradually through rental real estate.

It's not the cinch it used to be. The days of double-digit inflation are over. Tax breaks have been trimmed. Some rental markets are overbuilt. Units in strong markets are overpriced. But profits are still waiting to be made. All it takes is a plan and plenty of hard work.

I can't supply the work, but I would like to suggest a plan. Follow these steps, and you will be revered by your heirs:

1. Convert your first home to a rental when you move up.

2. When the property's market value has risen at least 20%, or when you have reduced the principal balance of your mortgage by 20%, take out a second mortgage to siphon off your increased equity. (The terrific feature of rentals is that your tenants are paying down your mortgage and building up equity.)

You should keep the equity in all of your rental properties reasonably low—first by making a small down payment, then by periodically remortgaging. The lower your equity, up to the point where it produces a negative cash flow, the higher your return on investment. For example, if you refinance to keep the equity in your $150,000 rental condominium at $20,000, your yield on a $4,000 profit will be 20% ($20,000 × 20% = $4,000). On the other hand, if you let the equity build up to $40,000, the return on your investment will be only 10% ($40,000 × 10% = $4,000).

3. Invest the tax-free cash you receive from refinancing as a down payment or partial payment on another single-family house or condominium.

4. Remortgage the second rental when your equity has increased at least 20% and begin to move up to larger properties by reinvesting the proceeds in a duplex (2-unit building).

5. Repeat the process of remortgaging one or all of your properties to buy more rentals. Work your way up to multi-unit apartment buildings if you're so inclined.

6. Hire a management company when handling the job yourselves becomes too time-consuming. Typical fees run from 8% to 10% of the rents collected.

While you are gleefully amassing properties, bear the tax law in mind, though. Generally, your deduction of rental losses is limited to $25,000. Even this allowance begins to phase out when your adjusted gross income tops $100,000. As few as two to four rentals can generate total losses (including paper losses from depreciation) of more than $25,000. Unless you have other passive income or your rentals quickly show a positive cash flow, you will receive no tax benefit from adding more and more properties. This will make them costlier to own.

Your best entrée into rental real estate is to rent out your first home when you move to posher quarters. As a starter house, it probably cost a lot less than comparable homes on the market right now. You should, therefore, be able to rent it for close to or more than your monthly mortgage payments, giving you an immediate positive cash flow.

Notice that I advocate buying a single-family house or condominium as your second rental, too. Why not think bigger? Because rental houses offer hard-to-beat advantages to individual investors:

- They practically manage themselves. As anyone who has been awakened at two in the morning by a tenant with plumbing problems will tell you, this is no mean feat. Tenant turnover is low. And day-to-day maintenance, such as cleaning and gardening, is usually done by the tenant. It's only one unit, too, not ten, so there are fewer things to go wrong. If they do, repairs can usually be taken care of with a phone call to a repairman.

- Homes are likely to appreciate more than apartments. And there is a broader market for them when it comes time to sell.
- Homes are easier to finance and to buy. Much smaller amounts of cash are needed to get started.
- Bargain-priced homes are easier to find. If you can find a seller motivated by financial problems, divorce, job transfer, or other pressures, you may be able to pick up a home at 10% to 15% below market value. Such pressures rarely force the sale of apartment buildings. The market for apartment buildings is also quite efficient, because prospective buyers can analyze a building's profits and accurately determine its value.

If single-family houses have virtue, condominiums are even better. In fact, they may be the ideal starter investment in rental real estate. Prices are less inflated, so you can draw tenants with more reasonable rent, and maintenance is almost nil. Why search for a low-cost old house that requires time and money to renovate and repair when you can buy a new condominium for a similar price? And the homeowner fees are fully deductible if the condominium is used as a rental.

If you do decide on a condominium, avoid one with restrictive owner regulations that limit your freedom to manage and rent. Buy the most popular floor plan, and stick to simple, familiar styles.

The Secret of Rental Success

It may not involve office politics, coffee breaks, or staff meetings, but a rental is a *business*. As a real estate entrepreneur, you must research and select properties critically, paying particular attention to the bottom line. Especially after tax reform, income should be your unwavering objective, even if you post losses in the early years. You also want the highest return possible from your investment. This comes from a combination of (1) rents, (2) tax benefits, and (3) appreciation.

Here's how you can achieve as much success in the rental business as you have in the nine-to-five world:

- **Establish your investment goals.** I know you want to make money. But give that desire some numbers. Do you want a 10% return on your rental investment? Do you want or need a monthly, positive cash flow of $100 right away? Or are you willing to go in the hole each month if the property has outstanding appreciation potential? If so, how much can you afford to pay out before the building pays off?

  Give some thought to the numbers involved in buying and selling. How much do you need to put down to achieve a positive cash flow? How big a mortgage payment can you support if the house is vacant for one or two months? When and under what conditions would you sell?

- **Know the market.** You're not just buying a building—you're buying a neighborhood. Learn all you can about comparable properties in the area, about rents, vacancy rates, and property taxes. Find out about rent control, redevelopment, and zoning. Pay attention to how well the area's largest employers are doing. Are businesses opening up or closing down? Check out the demographics, too: statistics on income, the number of persons in each household, and the direction of population growth.

- **Shop till you drop.** Don't let sheer laziness keep you from inspecting more than a handful of properties. Two seemingly identical properties can have dramatically different profit potentials. Or one may be selling at 10% below market and the other at 10% above. Besides, what better way to learn the market than by viewing what it has to offer?

- **Inspect properties closely.** You're not sightseers. You are searching for a profitable building. And a building that needs extensive repairs will be just the opposite. Turn on the faucets, throw back the rugs, test the washer and dryer. Estimate how much it will cost to spruce up the place and figure that into your offering price.

  Of course, some structural problems are invisible. When you have decided on a property, call in a house inspector. Expensive problems to correct: foundation cracks, corroded plumbing, and leaking roofs.

- **Manage wisely.** You don't need Harvard M.B.A.s, just common sense and attention to detail. Raise rents to profitable (and competitive) levels, minimize or reduce operating expenses, and maintain the appearance of the property. Screen tenants carefully, then keep them happy.

Buy the Numbers

When all is said and done, the crucial question is whether the investment makes economic sense. For the price you're paying, can you charge enough rent to cover all expenses? As prices rise, this is becoming a tougher standard to meet, and you may have to settle for a slight negative cash flow initially.

If the house is not currently rented, your math is simple. Add up your expected expenses—mortgage payments, insurance, property taxes, repairs, advertising, accounting, and utilities. If the total is $8,400, for example, ask whether you can get $700 a month in rent.

Where the property is already a rental, higher math takes over. There are several methods of income analysis, but the most popular and reliable is known as the **capitalization ("cap") rate.**

The cap rate is your yield—10% to 12% is what you should shoot for (never less than 7%). The cap rate is computed by dividing the property's net income (rent minus expenses) by the proposed purchase price.

Let's say you have found a property priced at $180,000, and the seller claims he nets $15,000. If you want a 10% yield on your investment, is the asking price reasonable? Dividing the net income of $15,000 by 10%, we find that you won't get your yield if the property costs more than $150,000. If the seller won't come down $30,000, you shouldn't buy.

What if you think you can boost net income by raising rents? How much would net income have to rise to yield 10%? Multiply the asking price of $180,000 by 10%, and we see that a net income of $18,000 is needed. You will have to raise rents by $3,000 ($250 a month).

The asking price is the most flexible figure in the computation, but you may decide to lower your expected yield in some cases—for example, if the property has exceptional appreciation potential.

Don't use any formula based on *gross* income. The problem with using gross income is that it fails to account for expenses. Always zero in on net income.

Fact-finding. The smartest formula in the world is no help without the right numbers—about the rent, operating expenses, and vacancy rate (5% is acceptable). Don't accept the seller's claims on faith. You have to be your own auditor. Ask to see the seller's tax schedule for that particular property. Then review the rent receipts, property tax bill, bank statements, and receipts for operating expenses. If the property has not been well maintained, add 5% of gross income to expenses.

Verification is vital. If a seller exaggerates rents by as little as 5%, it will reduce your yield by about 2% and cause some negative cash flow. If the seller balks at providing information, walk away.

If separating fact from fantasy overwhelms you, hire an accountant. Make sure you have a lawyer, too, to review sales documents and to help negotiate.

You may want an appraisal to confirm your opinion. This is especially useful for the purchase of a house not previously used as a rental.

Cash flow. After the cap rate, the before-tax cash flow is the most important number. Cash flow is simply what's left in your rental bank account after all expenses, including the mortgage, have been paid. Use this worksheet for your computation:

CASH FLOW WORKSHEET

1. Expected gross income $ _____
2. Times: Vacancy rate
   (vacancy losses/gross
   income)   × _____
3. Adjusted gross income   _____
4. Minus: Operating
   expenses
   a. Real estate taxes $ _____
   b. Insurance   _____
   c. Repairs   _____
   d. Trash collection   _____
   e. Advertising   _____
   f. Accounting   _____
   g. Utilities   _____
   h. Other   _____
                                   (_____)
5. Net operating income   _____
6. Minus: Mortgage
   payment
                                   (_____)
7. Cash flow   _____

TAX ASPECTS OF RENTAL REAL ESTATE

Perhaps no investment you make will personally involve you in as much tax law as rental real estate. Don't let that daunt you, however. The tax benefits are what make rentals such attractive investments. One of them is the ability to generate paper losses through depreciation. There is no finer thrill than claiming a deduction that never came near your wallet.

Rental Income and Expenses

Renting is a business, just like owning a mini-mart or a medical practice. It is unlike those businesses, however, because the income is **passive**—that is, you perform few or no services for your customers (tenants). For this reason, there are limitations on the amount of losses you can deduct. Because rentals are a specialized business, they have their own tax schedule, Schedule E, *Supplemental Income Schedule.*

Rental income. Rental income is taxable. Rent payments may be in the form of cash or property. Rent in the form of property, whether freezers or firewood, is included in income at its fair market value.

Normally, rental income consists of fixed amounts that you receive monthly from tenants. But there are other amounts that are considered rental income.

One of these is advance rent. If you require new tenants to pay both the first and last months' rent when they move in, the total is included in income in the year received. The same is true for prepaid rent.

A security deposit is *not* rent and should not be reported as income when received. If the tenant defaults, however, and you keep all or part of the deposit, you must report the amount in income in that year.

Under the terms of a lease, a tenant may agree to pay your operating expenses, such as maintenance, taxes, and utilities. Such an arrangement is called a **net lease,** and the payments are treated as additional rental income to you. You may then claim the deductible expenses (see below) to offset the income.

Rental expenses. As with any other business, you may deduct the operating expenses of your rental from your gross rental income. Only the net profit (or loss) is added to (or subtracted from) your other gross income.

The following are deductible rental expenses:

Accounting fees.

Advertising.

Automobile and travel to inspect your properties or to buy supplies. It is simplest to use the current standard mileage rate to compute your deduction.

Cleaning and maintenance.

Commissions paid to a management company. But commissions or other settlement costs paid to acquire the property must be capitalized, that is, added to the basis of your property.

Depreciation may be taken on the cost of the building (not the land). Use your property tax bill to determine how much of your cost is allocated to the building. Residential rental property must be depreciated over 27.5 years. The IRS publishes a depreciation table for ease of computation. The amount of depreciation you may claim depends on the month in which the property is first placed in service. Thus, the best time to buy a rental is in the first quarter of the year.

In addition, you may depreciate the cost of improvements, including remodeling, furniture, carpets, drapes, and appliances. These items are depreciated over seven years. Again, the IRS provides a table.

Insurance premiums for fire, liability, theft, and other disasters.

Gardening.

Homeowners' association dues. Extra assessments for capital expenditures, however, such as repaving or replacing pool furniture must be added to the basis of your property.

Interest on mortgages and other indebtedness.

Legal fees for evicting tenants or negotiating leases.

Office supplies and postage.

Real estate taxes. But special assessments for sewers, sidewalks, or other local improvements must be added to the basis of your property.

Repairs, such as repainting, mending fences, replacing missing tiles, or unclogging drains. If you personally make repairs to your property, you may not deduct the value of your labor or time.

Telephone and utilities.

Wages paid handymen or other maintenance or service employees.

Allocation for personal use. If you occupy a portion of your rental, the expenses attributable to your use of the property are personal and not deductible.

Note, however, that the personal portion of mortgage interest and taxes may be carried over to Schedule A, *Itemized Deductions,* if you are itemizing.

Passive Loss Rules

All rental activity is considered passive under the tax law. Losses from passive activities can only be used to offset passive income—for example, other rental gains or distributions from limited partnerships. Generally, passive losses cannot be used to offset active income, such as wages, or portfolio income, such as interest and dividends.

The good news is that active owners of rental property may deduct up to $25,000 in net rental losses ($12,500 married filing separate), whether or not they have passive income. Any excess net loss can be carried over.

You are an active owner if you make management decisions, such as approving tenants, setting rental rates, and authorizing repairs, even if you hire a management company to handle the day-to-day affairs. You cannot be an active owner if you are a limited partner or own less than a 10% interest in the rental.

Unfortunately, this $25,000 allowance is phased out at the rate of $1 for every $2 of adjusted gross income over $100,000 ($50,000 married filing separate). Investors with adjusted gross incomes over $150,000, therefore, can use rental deductions to offset only other rental or passive income.

Take heart, however. If you are ineligible to write off your passive losses, they may be carried forward to offset future passive income or to be deducted when the rental property is sold. *Tip:* By paying down the mortgage on one of your rentals, you might be able to turn a negative cash flow into a positive one that will enable you to absorb your other rental losses.

Installment Sales

The day may come when you want to sell. Perhaps the building has soared in value or perhaps it is almost fully depreciated. In any event, you expect a large taxable gain. One way to avoid paying the tax on the entire gain in the year of sale is to lend the buyer part of the purchase price. You can then elect to report your gain in the years the cash is actually received from the buyer. Thus, your tax is spread out in installments, just like the payments.

How can you qualify for this tax-saving treatment? All you need is an installment sale and the gain that comes with it. An installment sale occurs whenever you sell property and will receive one or more payments in a later year. That's it. At least two payments in different years.

POSSIBLE SOURCES
OF CASH FOR A DOWN PAYMENT

- Gift or shared-equity loan from parents or relatives
- Finding a cosigner for loan
- Renting with an option to buy
- Sale of personal assets or securities
- Loan secured by personal assets or securities
- Borrowing from 401(k) plan
- Withdrawal from retirement plan (subject to 10% penalty before age 59½)
- Cash value of life insurance
- Second mortgage from seller or other lender
- Lowering withholding allowances to increase take-home pay
- Low-down FHA or VA loan
- Doing repairs in exchange for lower down payment or sale price
- Asking real estate agent to take a note or I.O.U. for his commission instead of cash
- Using income tax refund as part of down payment
- Special loan assistance offered by employer
- Consolidation loan to reduce monthly payments on other debts
- Paying yourself extra rent each month (for example, if your actual rent is $750, budget $900 and deposit the extra $150 in a money market account)
- Taking a temporary second job
- Refinancing your automobile
- Accumulating more funds during escrow period
- Buying private mortgage insurance (covers the difference between 20% down and the lower amount you pay—as low as 5%)
- Obtaining a business loan to use for down payment
- Accepting a higher mortgage rate in exchange for lower "points" up front
- State financial aid for first-time buyers

7

TAX FOR TWO:
Tax Law for Married Couples

Tax and marriage. Not two words you probably link together. But more tax law hinges on marital status than any other factor. You may not realize it, but when you said "I do," you were consenting to pay tax for two. Taxes are a joint responsibility, as much a part of the marriage partnership as bringing up baby.

The tax effects of marriage depend in large part on which state you live in, which is why the next section deals with property laws. But first, let's find out what "married" means. You may think this is silly, because you already know what "married" means: legally hitched with a license, a mortgage, and diapers to prove it. You're right, of course. But as with all tax law, it's not quite that simple.

Your status as a married person is determined as of the last day of the year. You are considered married if, on the last day of the year, you are

1. married (license, mortgage, and all) and living together as husband and wife;

2. living together in a common-law marriage recognized in the state where it began or where you now live;

3. married and living apart, but not legally separated under a separate maintenance or divorce decree, or

4. separated under an interlocutory decree of divorce (issued for an interim period before the divorce becomes final).

Note that you do not have to be "legally" married—a common-law marriage qualifies (meaning that you have agreed to live together as husband and wife without benefit of a religious or civil ceremony). It must be recognized by state law, however. The states that sanction common-law marriages include Alabama, Alaska, Colorado, Connecticut, Florida, Georgia, Idaho, Iowa, Pennsylvania, Rhode Island, South Carolina, and Texas.

A common-law marriage begun in Georgia and continuing there for the required number of years will be recognized even if the couple later moves to California. But two people who begin to live together in California will not be considered married no matter how long they stay together, unless they move to one of the states that does recognize common-law marriage.

What if, through misfortune, your spouse dies during the year? Even though you are a widow or widower on the last day of the year, you are considered married for the entire year. If you do not remarry, you may file a joint return with your deceased spouse. If you do remarry before the end of the year, you may file a joint return with your new spouse.

COMMUNITY AND SEPARATE PROPERTY

Who owns your house, your car, your salary? The answer depends upon your state's property law, and it affects your taxes. There are two different state property systems in the United States. Most states follow a system based on the English common law and are known as **separate-property** states. Nine states, however, follow a **community property** system: Arizona, California, Idaho, Louisiana, Nevada, New Mexico, Texas, Washington, and Wisconsin are all community-property states. Federal income tax law recognizes both property systems.

Your domicile determines whether you have separate or community property and income. "Domicile" means your legal home. Like happiness, it is a state of mind. It is also the state in which you intend to have your permanent home, the place you always return to no matter how long or far you roam. You may have only one domicile, even though you may have several homes. A wife's domicile is generally that of her husband.

What are some of the factors the law looks to in considering domicile?

1. Where you were born
2. Where you pay state income tax
3. Where you vote
4. Where your car is registered and you hold a driver's license
5. The location of property you own
6. Length of residence

Consider Frank and Dorothy. They met and fell in love in their hometown in Ohio. Shortly after they married,

Frank's employer transferred him to Texas. Frank plans to go back to graduate school in Ohio in four years and to build his career there. Frank and Dorothy are domiciled in Ohio because they intend that state to be their permanent home.

The fact that Frank and Dorothy are domiciled in Ohio, a separate-property state, means that all the income they earn in Texas and the assets they acquire with that income are separate property, even though Texas is a community-property state. If, however, they had intended Texas to be their domicile, all income earned in Texas and the property bought with that income would have been community property.

What difference does it make? Plenty. Separate property belongs solely to the spouse who earns or acquires it. Community property is owned half by the husband and half by the wife, no matter who earns or acquires it. Married couples in community-property states may own both separate and community property, depending upon the source. Once property is classified as separate or community, it always retains that character, even if the couple later changes its domicile.

In *all* states, property acquired before marriage is separate property, as are inheritances or gifts, whether received before or after marriage. Property bought with separate property or bought in a separate-property state is also separate property in all states. Community property is all property not identifiable as separate property.

In a separate-property state, all wages or business profits earned by one spouse are the property of that spouse. The other spouse has no right to any part of them. The same is true for income earned by separate property, for example, stocks or an apartment building.

On the other hand, wages or business income earned in

one of the community-property states becomes the property of the "community" or marriage. The income is owned equally and jointly by each spouse. If the community were to dissolve, each spouse would be entitled to one-half of the community estate.

The treatment of income from separate property varies among community-property states. In Texas, Idaho, and Louisiana, income from separate property is community property. In the other community-property states, income from separate property is also separate property.

Can community property ever be converted into separate property or separate property into community property? Yes—by commingling or by using a prenuptial agreement.

Commingling

Commingling is, in effect, monetary stew. To concoct it, take a large pot, for example, a joint savings account, and toss in, first, community property, then income from separate property over a period of several years, all the time withdrawing money whenever necessary to run the household and feed the baby. Keep no records of deposits or withdrawals. Continue stirring the funds until the proceeds from the separate property are no longer identifiable. At that point, the entire savings account is community property.

Sometimes the conversion is not complete. This can happen, for example, when one spouse invests separate property in a house, along with an equal amount of community funds. Although the separate and community property have been commingled, in this case the amounts are easily traceable and identifiable. One-half the house is separate property and one-half is community property.

Prenuptial Agreement

Courtship and contracts would seem to conflict. Sometimes, however, a property agreement is wise. If you own substantial separate assets or there are children from a prior marriage, you may have entered into a prenuptial agreement with your spouse, defining each spouse's property rights.

A prenuptial agreement may provide, for example, that property acquired before and during marriage will remain separate property. Thus, Laura and Jim, domiciled in Washington, can make sure the money and stocks they brought to their marriage will not be commingled and lose their separate identity. Their salaries may also be kept separate, as well as any investments they make with their earnings. Laura and Jim must, however, treat their property as separate. If either allows her or his property to become untraceably commingled, it may be held to be community property in spite of the agreement.

Note that in most separate-property states, spouses may not agree to change their separate property to community property.

Property Laws and Your Tax Return

How do state property laws affect your tax return? By determining who reports income and who claims deductions. Your community paycheck is only half taxable to you. Those medical bills you paid with separate funds all go to reduce your separate income.

Tax treatment of community income after separation. The rule that each spouse in a community-property state must report one-half of the community income on his or her separate return can create an injustice if the couple is separated and no longer sharing income.

To temper this inequity, the tax law allows a separated spouse to report only his or her earnings if (1) the spouses lived apart for the entire calendar year; (2) one or both spouses had earned income during the year; *and* (3) no income, other than child support, was transferred between the spouses, either directly or indirectly.

MARRIED FILING?

The extent to which separate- and community-property laws affect your tax depends on the type of return you file. The returns for married couples come in two models: joint and separate. One model is not right for everybody, every year. Before you decide which is best for you, you must do some comparison shopping. In community-property states, the advantages of one over the other are usually minor, as we'll see below. In separate-property states, the differences can be substantial.

What do you look for in a joint or separate return? Let's define them first. Filing a joint return is like sleeping in a double bed—your income and expenses and your spouse's are added together and lie on the same 1040. You are two individual taxpayers, but you file only one return.

Filing a separate return, on the other hand, is like bunking in twin beds—your income and expenses lie on your own separate return and so do your spouse's. You file two separate and distinct returns marked "his" and "hers."

Joint versus Separate

Naturally you want to choose the model that produces the least tax. The only way to do this is by computing the tax using both methods. There's no simpler way. Some general rules do apply, though.

In most cases, a joint return results in less tax than separate returns. Why? Certain tax benefits, such as the child care credit (see page 164), the earned income credit, and the credit for the elderly may be claimed only on a joint return.

A joint return also has the effect of "splitting" the incomes of both spouses equally. Like a Smith and Wesson, the joint return is a great equalizer. By evening up differences in income, the joint return tends to moderate the overall tax liability better than separate returns do. Furthermore, the separate tax rates are slightly higher than the rates for joint returns.

But the tax scales tip in favor of separate returns where one spouse paid extremely high medical expenses out of a small, separate income. The reason, of course, is the 7.5% adjusted gross income limitation. On a combined income of $50,000, for example, medical expenses would have to exceed $3,750 before even one dollar could be deducted. But if the spouse with the highest medical bills earned only $10,000, any amount above $750 could be deducted on a separate return.

The same principle applies to miscellaneous itemized deductions, because of the 2% adjusted gross income limitation, and to uninsured casualty losses, which must exceed 10% of your adjusted gross income plus $100.

Separate returns also have an edge where one spouse suffered a net operating loss that would be absorbed or reduced by the income of the other spouse, leaving a smaller deduction to carry back or carry over.

If one advantage of a joint return is to equalize income, what happens when the taxable incomes of both you and your spouse are about the same? Both joint and separate returns will produce about the same tax. For that reason, in community-property states, where a married couple's income is considered equal by law, the tax would be the same whether joint or separate returns were filed.

Does that mean you lucky residents of community-property states never have to compute and compare the tax effects of filing joint versus separate? Not necessarily. If one or both of you also have separate income, the picture changes. Toss in separate income and expenses and your and your spouse's income and expenses are no longer equal. In that case, filing separate returns may be less costly. This situation arises if you marry in midyear or if you bring substantial separate property into the marriage.

Don't forget to consider the effect on state taxes, too. Some states let a two-earner couple file separately, although their federal return is joint.

Now let's explore the mechanics of filing each type of return.

The Joint Return

There are separate lines for both your name and your spouse's at the top of the Form 1040. Write your full names, not "Mr." and "Mrs." It is customary for the husband's name, social security number, and occupation to get top billing. If you choose to list the wife first, be consistent. Your account is entered on the IRS computer under the name and social security number given priority on the first joint return you file. Switch at a later date, and you will spend years snarled in red tape.

If you file a joint return, you cannot change to a separate return after the due date of the return has passed.

Signing the joint return. Unless a joint return is signed by both spouses, it is not considered a joint return. But what if both signatures are not possible? If your spouse is ill or injured, you may sign for him or her if you receive oral permission. Sign your spouse's name on the proper line and write underneath, "By ——— husband (or wife)." Then attach a statement, dated and signed by you, explaining why your spouse cannot sign and stating that he or she has agreed to let you sign on his or her behalf.

Suppose your spouse is simply away from home. Ask for an automatic extension to file (Form 4868) if contact seems doubtful.

The Separate Return

If you are filing separate returns, each of you must report only your own income, deductions, or credits. If you have children or other dependents, you may divide their exemptions in the way that creates the lowest combined tax. You cannot split an exemption in half, however.

Each of you must also claim the actual amount withheld from your wages, unless you live in a community-property state. In that case, each of you takes credit for half of the taxes withheld from each other's paychecks, just as you each report half of your combined community income.

You must show both your spouse's name and social security number on your separate return in the space provided.

If one spouse itemizes deductions, the other spouse must also itemize. This requirement could make filing separate less advantageous than filing joint, when one spouse has few or no itemized deductions and thus loses the benefit of the standard deduction. If you do not itemize and later wish to (or vice versa), you may amend your separate returns, but both of you must make the same changes. You both must also file a consent to any additional tax that may be due as a result of the changes.

If you file a separate return, you may later change it to a joint return. This may be done at any time within three years of the due date of the separate returns.

You each sign your own separate returns. Write "Community-Property Split" on the bottom of the Form 1040 and Schedule A if you live in a community-property state.

The Marriage Penalty

Two may be able to live more cheaply than one, but they certainly pay more tax. Not surprising, I hear you say, because they probably earn twice as much. True. But married couples don't simply pay twice as much tax on twice as much income as single taxpayers. They pay up to 225% as much.

For example, Mona and Carl are two unmarried individuals, each with a taxable income of $30,000. Filing single returns, each would pay $5,879 in tax, or a combined total of $11,758 (based on the 1990 tax rates).

Jack and Betty are married, and each of them also has a taxable income of $30,000. Filing a joint return, their tax, on the same amount of income, would be $12,582, or 107% of the amount paid by Mona and Carl.

This additional tax is called the **marriage penalty,** and many couples think it is unfair and discriminatory. A marital deduction designed to alleviate this inequity was repealed in 1986.

What can you do to avoid the marriage penalty? At present, only one thing: avoid marriage. If that sounds too drastic, many of your fellow citizens don't agree. My clients frequently ask, in all sincerity, whether they should get a divorce and live together, rather than pay the marriage penalty. It has, of course, been done before. As far as I know, if you stay divorced, your single status cannot be legally questioned.

Some couples, however, want their lower tax and marriage, too. Typically, they fly off to some Caribbean isle in December, sever their bonds of matrimony, and fly home to a new wedding ceremony in January. These on-again, off-again marriages are fraught with legal perils, though. Your quickie Caribbean divorce may not be honored under your state's law; the divorce will then be invalid, and you will be considered married at the end of the year by the IRS. So if flyaway divorce appeals to you, please consult a lawyer first.

EXEMPTIONS

It's nice to count for something. So you'll be happy to know that you are worth $2,150 (indexed for inflation) to your government—dead or alive. This is not a bounty. It is the amount you can deduct on your tax return simply for having drawn breath at least one day during the year.

This allowance is called your **personal exemption.** You may take a personal exemption for yourself. So can your spouse. Your spouse is never your dependent. On a joint return, you both claim your own personal exemptions. If you file separate returns, you and your spouse will each take your personal exemptions on your own returns.

Phase-out of Personal Exemptions

The tax benefits of your personal and dependency exemptions begin to phase out at a certain level of income (the amount varies annually).

If you are filing separate, your tax liability from the phase-out is computed as if you were claiming an exemption for your spouse. This is to prevent you from avoiding the full effect of the phase-out by filing a separate return.

Exemptions for Children and Other Dependents

Aside from your personal exemptions, you may also take exemptions for your children and other dependents. If your dependent was either born alive or died during the year, you may take the full exemption. State law determines whether a child was born alive.

As the name implies, a dependent is someone who depends on you for support, but there is more to this innocent-sounding concept than that. In the tax law, even a baby is not a dependent until he meets five tests: (1) gross income test; (2) member of household or relationship test; (3) support test; (4) joint return test; and (5) citizenship test.

Gross income test. A dependent's gross income must be less than the exemption amount. Gross income is all income that is not exempt from tax, for example, your child's own earnings or interest paid by custodian accounts in your child's name.

Of course, most children, having little or no income, easily pass the gross income test. But what if your child is a financial prodigy? No problem. The test does not apply if your child is either:

1. under the age of 19, or
2. a full-time student (under age 24 for the entire tax year).

Your "child" is your son, daughter, stepdaughter, stepson, a legally adopted child, or a foster child who lived with you all year.

To qualify as a full-time student, your child must be enrolled full-time at a recognized school for at least five months of the year (not necessarily consecutively).

Attending school only at night is not full-time. Neither are correspondence courses or employee training programs. High school students who work in private industry as part of their school's vocational training are considered full-time students.

Member of household or relationship test. Your child or other relative does not have to live with you. Being a relative is enough. The one mysterious exception is a cousin. Your cousin is required to be a member of your household. Further, the relationship stemming from marriage is not ended by divorce or death. Your sister-in-law is still related to you long after your spouse remarries or passes away.

A legally adopted child is always considered your child, but a foster child must be a member of your household for the entire year. If you receive payments from a child placement agency as a foster parent, you may not take the child as a dependent.

You may also claim an exemption for a dependent who is not related to you if he was a member of your household for the entire year, and the other four tests are met.

Support test. More than one person can provide support for a dependent, including the dependent himself. But the winner of the exemption is the person who provides more than 50% of that support. If no one person contributed over half of the dependent's total support or if the person who did cannot take the exemption because of failure to meet the member of household or relationship test, it is possible no one will be entitled to take the exemption at all.

For example, if you provide over half the support of your indigent cousin in Tennessee, you may not claim his exemption, because a cousin must live with you. Your cousin, who has no taxable income and is not filing a return, cannot take his own exemption, either. Therefore, the exemption is lost.

Total support is the sum of

1. the fair rental value of lodging;
2. expenses paid for the dependent alone;
3. the dependent's share of expenses paid for the entire household of which the dependent is a member.

Dollars and cents are all that count. If you did not provide more than 50% of the dependent's total support, it does not matter that you were paying his or her expenses for a longer period of time than someone else.

Typical items of support include food, shelter, clothing, medical and dental care, medical insurance premiums, school tuition, child care expenses, personal grooming, recreation, gifts to the dependent, and transportation.

Items *not* included in support are life insurance premiums, Medicare benefits, income tax and social security tax paid by the dependent from his own income, funeral expenses, scholarships received by your child who is a full-time student (this also applies to tuition, room, and board provided to a handicapped or retarded child at a special school or institution), and a student nurse's room and board at an accredited school of nursing.

All the amounts paid for a dependent's total support must be tallied. If the dependent lived with you, such expenses as food, rent, and utilities must be divided by the number of persons who were members of your household to determine the dependent's share. Once you have arrived at the sum of the dependent's total support for the year, compare the amount contributed by the dependent for his own support with the amount you and others contributed. If you gave over 50% of the total, you may claim the exemption.

Remember that although we count only taxable income for the gross income test, all sources of income, both taxable and nontaxable, are taken into account in computing the amount spent for a dependent's support.

You do not have to include income that the dependent received and saved. A dependent is not required to spend any part of his income for his own support.

Support test for divorced or separated parents. When exemptions are spoils of marital wars, a special rule applies. Instead of looking to total support, this rule turns on custody.

Beginning in 1985, the tax law conclusively presumes that the parent who has custody furnished over 50% of each child's support and is, therefore, entitled to the exemption in all cases if

1. both parents together provided over half of the child's support during the calendar year, and
2. one or both parents had custody of the child for more than half of the calendar year, and
3. the parents are divorced or separated under a written agreement or lived apart during the last six months of the calendar year.

Custody is determined either by the most recent court decree or written separation agreement or, in its absence, by who had actual physical custody for the greater number of days during the year.

The only way a noncustodial parent may claim the exemption after 1984 is if the custodial parent signs a written declaration waiving her or his rights to the exemption. The noncustodial parent must attach this declaration, Form 8332, to his or her tax return each year the exemption is claimed.

Pre-1985 decrees or agreements. The general rule outlined above does not apply if a court decree or written separation agreement executed before January 1, 1985, expressly awards the exemption to the noncustodial parent *and* he or she pays at least $600 per year for each child's support. In that case, the noncustodial parent receives the exemption, regardless of whether the custodial parent provided 50% or more of the child's support and can prove it.

Joint return test. When you give away the bride, you lose more than a daughter. You lose a dependent. You may not take an exemption for your otherwise dependent child if she or he files a joint return.

If, however, the newlyweds are not required to file because of low earnings—for example, because they are full-time students—and only do so to claim a refund of withholding, you may take the exemption for either or both of them if the other four tests are met.

Citizenship test. Your dependent must be a U.S. citizen, resident, or national, or a resident of Canada or Mexico for some part of the year.

Children are normally considered citizens or residents of their parents' country. The child of a U.S. citizen may be recognized as a U.S. citizen for tax purposes, although the other parent was a nonresident alien and the child was born in a foreign country.

If you are living abroad and have legally adopted a child who is not a U.S. citizen or resident, you may claim the child as your dependent if he or she was a member of your household (which was the child's principal home) for the entire year.

CHILD AND DEPENDENT CARE CREDIT

If the cost of child care sometimes makes you wonder why both of you are working, let the tax law ease your mind. The child and dependent care credit allows you to deduct a percentage of your child care expenses directly from your tax. You do not have to itemize your deductions to claim this tax benefit.

Note that this credit also covers the cost of tending others besides children—disabled spouses and other dependents who cannot be left alone.

To qualify for the credit, your dependent care expenses must be incurred to enable you to work, whether full- or part-time or in your own business or partnership. The work must produce income. Volunteer work does not qualify.

You must also be paying over half the upkeep on a home or apartment that is the principal home of your dependent. The cost of maintaining a home includes mortgage payments or rent, real estate taxes, home insurance, home repairs, utility bills, and food. If your dependent care expenses cover a period of less than a year, you must prorate the annual upkeep over the number of months you paid for dependent care.

Your payments must be to someone who is not your dependent or child under age 19. You must file a joint return to claim the credit.

Qualifying Individuals

Your work-related expenses must be for the care of one or more of the following individuals:

1. Your dependent child under the age of 13, whom you are entitled to claim as an exemption

2. Your spouse who is physically or mentally unable to care for himself or herself

3. Your dependent of any age who is physically or mentally incapable of self-care

If your child turns 13 during the year, you may take a credit for the expenses incurred before his or her thirteenth birthday.

Qualifying Expenses

Before you pack your child off to boarding school or hire someone to cook and clean, let's examine what types of dependent care qualify for the credit. The care must be for the dependent's protection and well-being. Amounts paid for education and food, therefore, do not qualify unless these amounts cannot be separated from the cost of the care.

Expenses must be allocated if the cost includes education in the first grade or higher. For example, Tiffany is in the third grade at a private elementary school. For $2,500, Tiffany is taught about the Mayflower and math, served lunch, and allowed to stay after school. Only that part of the cost that is for Tiffany's care after school hours qualifies for the credit.

Care furnished outside the home qualifies only if the expense was for the care of your child under the age of 13. If your spouse or dependent is disabled, expenses must be for services performed in your home (unless the dependent regularly spends at least eight hours a day in your home, in which case the expenses can be incurred outside the home).

A day-care center, day camp, nursery school, baby-sitter's home, or boarding school may all qualify, although the expense must be reduced by tuition for a child in the first grade or higher. A dependent care center must comply with state and local law.

The cost of sending your child to an *overnight* camp no longer qualifies.

Transportation costs between your home and a dependent care facility are not qualifying expenses.

Expenses paid for domestic services in your home qualify if the work is done partly for the care and well-being of the qualifying person. This is true even though the duties include cleaning, cooking, and other household chores.

Add the cost of meals your housekeeper ate in your home to your dependent care expenses. If you incurred extra expenses for your housekeeper's lodging, they may also be counted.

Note: If you pay wages for services performed in your home, you may be liable for employment taxes (see below).

Amount of Credit

The tax law places two limitations on the amount of the credit: an earned income limit and a dollar limit.

Earned income limit. The amount of dependent care expenses you use to compute the credit cannot exceed your earned income. Earned income is figured without regard to community-property laws, that is, you may not count your community half of your spouse's earned income as your own.

Dollar limitation. The dollar limitation is actually two separate restrictions. First, your expenses are limited to

1. $2,400 for one qualifying individual;
2. $4,800 for two or more qualifying individuals.

If your child becomes 13 during the year, you do not prorate the $2,400 limitation.

The second dollar limitation is on the amount of the credit itself. The credit ranges from 20% to 30%. The exact percentage depends on your income. If your adjusted gross income is $10,000 or less, you may claim the maximum percentage of 30%. The credit then drops 1% for each $2,000 of adjusted gross income over $10,000, until it reaches the minimum credit of 20% at incomes above $28,000. The maximum credit for two children is $1,440 ($4,800 × 30%); the minimum credit is $960 ($4,800 × 20%).

The dependent care credit is subtracted from your tax liability. Use Form 2441 to claim your credit.

You must enter your day-care provider's name, address, and tax identification number. Failure to provide this information may result in disallowance of the credit. Ask your provider for a copy of Form W-10, showing this information.

Rules for Divorced or Separated Couples

The credit is available to married couples only if they file a joint return. You may, however, claim the credit on a separate return if

1. you and your spouse did not live together during the last six months of the tax year;

2. you maintain a household that is the principal residence of your dependent for more than half of the taxable year, and

3. you furnish over half the cost of maintaining the household for the year.

Your child need not be your dependent if the reason you are not entitled to the exemption is because you waived the right to claim it or because the exemption is being claimed by your ex-spouse under the provisions of a pre-1985 divorce or separation agreement.

If you are divorced or separated under a decree of separate maintenance, you may claim the credit only if you had custody for the greater part of the year. The child does not have to be your dependent. For instance, suppose your daughter lived with you for seven months during the year, but your ex-spouse provided over half her support. Even though your ex-spouse is entitled to the exemption because he provided the most support, you may nevertheless claim a child care credit because you had custody for more than six months.

Employment Taxes of Household Employees

If you pay a household employee—even a baby-sitter—wages of $50 or more in a quarter, the wages are subject to social security tax. You may deduct your employee's share from wages, or you may pay the entire tax yourself. (Any of the employee's share you pay must be added to his or her income on Form W-2, however.)

Social security tax is reported and paid quarterly using Form 942. File Form 942 starting with the first quarter you either pay wages subject to social security tax or withhold income tax from wages at your employee's request.

If you pay cash wages of $1,000 or more per quarter, you are also liable for federal unemployment tax. This tax is paid entirely by you. File Form 940 by January 31 of the year following the close of the year for which the tax is due.

Your share of employment taxes is not deducted, but is added to your other dependent care expenses in figuring your credit.

What if you suspect the wages are not being reported to the IRS because your child care provider insists on being paid in cash and refuses to tell you her social security number? What if you don't even claim the child care credit because you don't want to get your sitter in trouble and because good child care providers are hard to come by?

I sympathize. But the worries and frustrations of finding suitable day care don't sway the IRS. You are liable for employment taxes whether or not your sitter reports the income or you claim the child care credit. The cost of noncompliance, if the IRS finds out, is steep. Besides the unpaid tax, you face a penalty equal to *100%* of the total tax—plus interest on both the tax and penalty. And there's a remote possibility that criminal charges could be brought.

Consider these legal implications carefully before letting loyalty for your child care provider overcome your best interests.

TAX WITHHOLDING AND ESTIMATED TAX

Two-earner couples face a unique problem—underwithholding. It's another form of the marriage penalty discussed above. Because the withholding on your paycheck is based on just one salary, it isn't adequate to cover the tax when that salary is combined with your spouse's income.

To avoid an underpayment penalty, you have four choices. You may

1. claim fewer withholding allowances (however, zero is as low as you can go);

2. ask your employers to withhold an additional amount;

3. check the box "Married, but withhold at higher Single rate" on Form W-4;

4. make estimated tax payments.

Estimated tax is the amount of your total tax not covered by withholding or tax credits. You *must* pay estimated tax if that amount is $500 or more for the year and you had a federal tax liability for the previous year. Estimated tax is paid quarterly, beginning April 15, using Form 1040-ES. If you fail to make required estimated tax payments, you are liable for an underpayment penalty.

SELF-EMPLOYMENT INCOME AND TAX

The mom-and-pop grocery store may be a nostalgic reminder of more innocent times, but many married couples still operate family-owned businesses. The tax question to which such businesses give rise is which spouse reports the income and pays the self-employment (social security) tax.

Even though you consider the business a "partnership," if either you or your spouse exercises substantially all the management and control, then all the income and deductions are treated as that spouse's and only that spouse is liable for self-employment tax. This holds true even though for income tax purposes the income is attributed to both of you because you live in a community-property state.

Because self-employment tax can be greater if paid by two spouses each reporting one-half the income than by one spouse reporting it all, some couples claim that the husband (usually) is a sole proprietor and that the wife helps out occasionally without pay because she is a model spouse.

This strategy has several shortcomings. If the husband and wife actually share the job of carrying on the business and their tax return is audited, this misrepresentation is likely to look like tax evasion (if underpayment resulted) and can lead to costly penalties. Potentially even more costly to the wife is that by not paying her half of the self-employment tax, she is being deprived of social security credits. That may not seem important right now, if you are young and confident of success and a long-standing marriage. Suffice it to say that life is unpredictable.

If you and your spouse actually operate as a partnership under a written agreement, you should report your business's profit (or loss) on Form 1065, *U.S. Partnership Return of Income*. But, unlike your Form 1040, the partnership return is an "information" return only. This means that your share of the partnership's net earnings are passed through to your joint or separate returns, where you pay tax on it.

If your "partnership" is in spirit rather than in writing, you can simplify your tax life by reporting earnings as sole proprietors on your Form 1040. Use two Schedule Cs to report your respective shares of the profit (or loss).

LIABILITY FOR TAX

Both you and your spouse are liable, jointly and *individually*, for the tax and any penalties due on your joint return. This means that you may be held responsible for paying the entire tax, even though your spouse earned part of the income. By contrast, if you file separately, you are liable for only the tax due on your own return.

Because the IRS can collect the full tax from one of you alone if you file a joint return, it is vital that both of you examine and understand every item on the return before signing. If you have any doubt about whether the joint return is correct, file your own separate return instead.

This joint liability extends to audit deficiencies and penalties for negligence and fraud. Nonetheless, relief from fraud may be granted to an innocent spouse under narrow circumstances.

Innocent Spouse Rule

The tax law contains an "innocent spouse" rule. Under its provisions, a spouse will not be held liable for tax and penalties if

1. there is an underpayment of tax on the joint return in excess of $500 due to the omission of gross income by the other spouse or deductions or credits claimed by the other spouse (provided the innocent spouse's own tax liability exceeds a certain amount discussed below);

2. the innocent spouse did not know or had no reason to know that income was omitted or deductions or credits were not allowable;

3. after considering all facts and circumstances, it would be inequitable to hold the innocent spouse liable.

You cannot claim lack of knowledge because you signed a blank return or claim ignorance of the law if your spouse was no more knowledgeable than you. If you are both "innocent," you are both liable.

Spouses have also been held liable when they made no effort to ascertain the correct income, even though they had been put on notice by their spouse's refusal to answer their questions about income. In these cases, the spouses had access to the books and records.

Innocent spouses must also show that they did not significantly benefit from their spouse's fraud. The benefit must be more than ordinary support. One wife was found to have significantly benefited when the omitted income was spent on improvements to the home, a swimming pool, vacations, and automobiles. She also had $17,500 tucked away in a personal savings account. This is a subjective test and varies from case to case.

Limitation based on tax liability. The innocent spouse rule does not apply unless the innocent spouse's tax liability attributable to unallowable deductions or credits exceeds $500 and a certain percentage of adjusted gross income for the year before the tax deficiency notice was mailed. If the innocent spouse's adjusted gross income was $20,000 or less, the underpayment must exceed 10% of such adjusted gross income; for adjusted gross incomes over $20,000, it must exceed 25%.

If the innocent spouse has remarried as of the end of the preceding year, the new spouse's income must be included in the adjusted gross income of the innocent spouse.

Community property and the innocent spouse rule. The IRS may disregard community-property rules and tax a spouse on any income that the spouse treated as his or hers alone, if the other spouse was not notified of the nature and amount of the income before the due date of the return.

In addition, a spouse who files a separate return may be relieved of tax liability on community income earned by the other spouse if (1) he or she does not know about the community income, and (2) it would be inequitable to tax the unsuspecting spouse on such income.

Fraud or duress. Besides the innocent spouse rule, you are not liable for a joint return if it was signed as a result of fraud, trickery, or duress.

To assert the defense of duress, you must show that you were unable to resist your spouse's demand that you sign and that you would not have signed except for this constraint on your will. Generally, you must show that you feared physical abuse because of your spouse's threats. The threat must have been present when you signed, however. If your spouse threatens you, but you do not sign until the next day, when he or she is not around, you cannot claim duress.

If your spouse forges your signature on a joint return, you are not liable. The same is true if you sign a return believing it is a separate return on the assurance of your spouse.

INJURED SPOUSE CLAIM

The IRS can apply all or part of a refund to past-due child and spousal support or federal non-tax debts, such as your student loans. But if the IRS takes a refund due on a joint return to pay your spouse's obligation, you may file a claim for your share of the joint overpayment if

1. you are not also obligated for the past-due amount;
2. you received and reported income on the joint return;
3. you made and reported tax payments (for example, withholding or estimated tax) on the joint return.

To receive your share of the refund, complete Form 8379 and Form 1040X, through item d. Social security numbers must be in the same order as they appear on the joint return. Write "Injured Spouse" on top of the Form 1040X.

An injured spouse claim can be made when you file your regular return. Attach Forms 1040X and 8379 to the front of your Form 1040 below the name and address area.

$ $ $

As we've seen, your marital status has far-reaching effects on your tax liability. The information in this chapter can help you to take advantage of the tax savings available to couples and to sidestep tax traps. Let me stress again, however, how important it is for both of you to have a working knowledge of the tax law. Of all financial duties, taxes most often seem to fall on the same spouse year-in and year-out. But what if that spouse becomes sick or disabled or you decide to divorce?

On the lighter side, what if your designated tax hero is really quaking in his or her boots when he or she goes up against your tax return? Why should one of you have to face the 1040 alone? After all, marriage is more than sharing the good times. Joining forces against the tax dragon may draw you closer together. It certainly will make you a dynamite financial team.

8

PIGGY BANKING: Your Child's Finances

Tiptoe into the nursery. That tiny being in the crib is completely dependent on you. To diaper, feed, and manage his money. Money? Yes. Dr. Spock may have overlooked it, but the day that baby comes home, a two-earner couple often becomes a three-earner family. Even if your child wasn't born with a silver spoon in his mouth, he was probably given at least a savings bond or two. From the moment he drew his first breath, he was earning interest.

That's not all. Grandparents will rush to open savings accounts and buy stock in the toddler's name. You will, of course, set up a college fund. Then there will be today's equivalent of a lemonade stand. Your bundle of joy may even display a talent for making a bundle—as a rock star or a junior Rockefeller.

Your child may also profit from your own estate and tax planning. I know babies who could boast of complex trusts and off-shore corporations—if they were only old enough to talk. Their parents spend more time engineering their children's finances than they do their own.

Unfortunately, money attracts taxes. Age is no defense.

176

As soon as investment income nudges past $550, Daddy's little exemption becomes Mommy's little taxpayer—even if she has to sign his name in finger paint. The three Rs since tax reform have been reading, write-offs, and 'rithmetic. So if you're searching for a bedtime story, trade Mother Goose for Uncle Sam. Just remember to leave a night-light on. That's a Grimm fairy tale if ever there was one.

In this chapter, we explore strategies for transferring wealth to your child, as well as your child's monetary rights. We also take a look at laws governing the working child and the fringe benefits that can come with a paycheck. Finally, we discuss your child's tax return and how to keep the IRS from raiding the piggy bank. Like many parents, you will probably prepare your child's return; it's rarely economical to farm it out to a professional preparer. The Herculean labor of saving and investing for your child's college education is covered in Chapter 9.

THE GIFT THAT KEEPS ON GIVING

Dolls lose arms, softballs unravel. But cash keeps growing greener. Beyond that, there are sound estate and tax-planning reasons to give assets, as well as playthings, to your child. Not to mention the freedom of choice even the most modest trust fund offers at the start of adult life.

The IRS does not rap gifts. You and your spouse may give up to $10,000 apiece to each child (a combined $20,000) annually without paying gift tax. Even gifts above this amount may escape tax: the unified estate and gift tax law allows each of you a lifetime exemption of $600,000 on transfers made by gift or by will, above and beyond the annual $10,000 limit. There is also no limit on gifts paid for your child's tuition or medical expenses. The only requirement is that the money be paid directly to the school or health-care provider.

Gifts in excess of the $10,000 per person annual exclusion must be reported on Form 709, *Gift Tax Return,* and a credit against the gift tax computed.

If you and your spouse join together to give between $10,000 and $20,000, you must file Form 709A (unless the gift was community property). No tax is due, but you must make an election to act jointly.

Both Forms 709 and 709A are due by April 15 of the year after the gift was made. Don't forget that you live in a republic. Check your state's gift tax law—it may be stricter than the federal.

I am constantly consulted by worried donees, convinced that the gift of several thousand dollars they received is a tax bomb their relative tossed before it could go off. The truth is, the only gifts that tick are clocks. The gift tax, if any, is imposed on the donor. The gift, therefore, will not be reported on your child's tax return. But any interest, dividends, or capital gains that the gift earns are taxable to him.

WHAT IS A GIFT?

You can give cash, securities, real estate, collectibles, a share of your business. Form does not make a gift—it's your intent and the fact that there is no consideration. That is, you do not expect a payment in return.

There is one exception: The forgone interest on a low- or no-interest loan is considered a gift subject to gift tax. Forgone interest is the difference between the interest actually charged and the interest that would be collected using a rate set by the federal government (the applicable federal rate). *Note:* Low- or no-interest loans of $10,000 or less are exempt from gift tax unless used to purchase income-producing property, such as rental real estate. The same is true for interest-free loans of up to $100,000 if your child's net investment income for the year is $1,100 or less. (Net investment income equals gross investment income minus $1,100 if your child does not itemize his deductions. If he does itemize, net investment income equals gross investment income minus the larger of [1] $1,100 or [2] $550 plus itemized deductions that are directly connected with the production of the investment income.)

An interest-free loan lets you make a short-term gift of income and still get the principal back without the legal acrobatics of setting up a trust. For example, suppose you lend your son $80,000 at no interest. If he invests that $80,000 at 8%, it will earn $6,400 a year. In effect, you are making an annual gift of $6,400 to him. But it costs you less than making an outright gift of $6,400. That's because you would have to pay tax on the $6,400 before you gave it to your son if you invested the $80,000 yourself. If you are in the highest tax bracket (31%), it would cost you $9,275 to make a $6,400 gift ($9,275 minus tax of 31%). With an interest-free loan, your son will pay the tax (and he may be in a lower bracket). You won't owe gift tax, either, because the forgone interest amounts to less than the annual exclusion of $10,000 in this case. Best of all, you will get your $80,000 back when the note comes due.

Make sure that you have an enforceable loan note, though, or the IRS may treat the entire loan as a gift, instead of just the forgone interest.

Other, less common, gifts include forgiving debts, changing title of separately owned property to joint tenancy, and transferring assets to a family partnership or closely held corporation. Assigning ownership to another person in a life insurance contract which has cash value or paying premiums on a policy owned by someone else is also treated as a gift.

THE ART OF GIVING

You can make a gift to your child outright or put the property in trust. Generally, gifts in trust, however, do not qualify for the $10,000 annual exclusion. There are two exceptions: a minor's trust and a Crummey trust (discussed on page 187).

In most cases, all you need to make a gift are ribbons and bows. Simply handing over the asset makes your child the owner. Some legal groundwork must be laid, however, if the property has a written document of title. A car, for example, must be registered in the donee's name. If it is a car you already own, this means a trip to your state's motor vehicle department. Otherwise, the dealer from whom you are buying will handle the title change.

Stock in publicly traded corporations must show your child as the new record owner. Let your stockbroker grapple with the paperwork. If you are giving stock that you own in a closely held corporation, you must sign the back of your certificate to cancel your shares and surrender it to the company's Secretary, who will issue a new certificate to your child.

Real estate wins the red tape award. A new deed must be drawn up and recorded. Title and insurance policies must be amended or reissued. If there is an unassumable mortgage on the property, you must secure the lender's consent to the gift or risk having to pay off the mortgage balance.

INCOME SPLITTING

Love aside, tax savings are the primary reason parents give to their children. Savings for college or other future needs grow faster when you shift them to your child, because the income they produce is taxed at your child's rate, not at your presumably higher one.

Unfortunately, tax reform has stripped income splitting of the bonanza tax benefits they once enjoyed. By taxing some of your child's income at your top tax rate and by narrowing the spread between the lowest and the highest tax brackets, Congress has taken some of the profit, if not the pleasure, out of giving.

Although income splitting has been devalued, it is still a valid strategy. Assuming a yield of 10%, your child under 14 could have $11,000 in assets and not be taxed at your rate. At age 14 or older, your child could have $203,500 invested at 10% without being pushed out of the 15% bracket (using 1991 Tax Rates). If you are in the top tax bracket, shifting taxable income of $1,100 to your child will save you $258 in taxes per child, per year.

To benefit, however, you must permanently transfer, not just income, but the property that earns it. Unless you actually give up ownership to your child, any income is taxable to you.

Merely transferring legal title is not enough. You must give up all use and control as well. Two accepted ways of surrendering ownership—custodian accounts and trusts—

are discussed below. The best device for you depends on your child's age, the amount of money or property, and when you want your child to have the use of it.

CUSTODIAN ACCOUNTS

You don't hand a two-year-old $10,000. A teddy bear, yes. But not cash. The same is true, perhaps more so, at age 10 or 15. Unless you want to own a video arcade or a trainload of heavy metal albums.

What you really want to do is give the money now, but the use of it later. In law, this is known as giving a **future interest.** How do you go about it? Either buy a time machine, or simpler, make use of the Uniform Gifts to Minors Act (UGMA) or the Uniform Transfer to Minors Act (UTMA). These acts permit you to open bank or brokerage accounts for your child. Your child has legal title to the funds or securities in the account, but it is administered by a custodian for your child's benefit.

Gifts under UGMA are limited to cash, securities, and in some states, life insurance and annuities. You can transfer a wider range of assets to an UTMA, including real estate, patents, royalties, and paintings. Note that you cannot give securities you hold on margin. Property that your child already owns cannot be placed in a custodian account. The gift must be a current one.

You can't make a single gift to more than one child. For example, you can't give a block of 500 shares of stock jointly to your son and your daughter. You can break up the block and give 250 shares to Johnny in his name and 250 to Jenny in hers.

The custodian may be a parent, grandparent, brother,

sister, uncle, aunt, or guardian. Only one custodian may be named. You and your spouse cannot share the responsibility. In some states, the custodian may be any adult, bank, or trust company.

If you are both the donor and the custodian, the assets in the account will be taxed as part of your estate if you die. It is wise, therefore, to name your spouse as custodian if you make the gift, and vice versa.

The custodian has considerable discretion in managing the gift. He or she can make investment decisions, such as to buy (but not on margin) or sell securities in the account and to collect and distribute income. The only restriction is that his or her actions be considered prudent.

The capital in the account may be spent for your child's support, maintenance, education, or other benefit. But if any income from the investment is used for support, it will be taxable to you. Otherwise it is taxed to your child. What constitutes support? Any expense that you are required to provide your child under state law—for example, food, shelter, clothing, or medical care.

The first step in setting up a custodian account is to obtain a social security number for your child. Make sure this number is shown as the "owner" of the account.

Do not open a bank account or buy stock certificates in both your name and your child's as joint tenants or tenants in common. In that case, one-half of the earnings or capital gains would be taxable to you. Worse still, a U.S. savings bond purchased in your names would be fully taxable to you, because you contributed the money.

Income on a U.S. savings bond, bank account, or stock certificate in your child's name alone will be taxable to him, even if you are named as the beneficiary.

In the 23 states that permit UGMAs, all principal and accumulated income in the custodian account must be distributed to your child when he reaches 18. With UTMA, which 27 states and the District of Columbia have adopted, distribution can be postponed until age 21 (age 25 in California). No formal accounting is needed unless requested by your child. Generally, the custodian is not liable for any losses unless caused by bad faith, gross negligence, or intentional wrongdoing.

Factors to Consider

What are some of the pros and cons of a custodian account? As we've already discussed, the income from the account will be taxed to your child. In the past, this usually meant that it was taxed at a lower rate. No thanks to tax reform, however, unearned income in excess of $1,000 received by your child before he turns 14 is now taxed at your top rate.

Your strategy, therefore, should be to set up a gift-giving program that holds interest and dividend income below $1,100 until your child reaches age 14. That way, the tax won't exceed 15%. For example, assuming a 10% yield, you could give your child under 14 up to $11,000 ($11,000 × 10% = $1,100) without being taxed at your rate.

Alternatively, you can make gifts of property that earn tax-free or tax-deferred income or that won't mature until your child is 14—for example, growth stock. If your child won't reach 14 for five years, consider U.S. savings bonds, Series EE, which have a guaranteed yield of 6% if held for six years. They are not subject to state tax and no federal tax is due until the bonds are cashed in—by which time your child will be taxed at his own rate.

Other investments that defer income are life insurance, single-premium annuities, municipal bonds, and deep discount (zero-coupon) bonds that mature when your child reaches age 14 or enters college.

Once your child is 14 or older, you can step up the amount of your gift giving and switch to certificates of deposit, money market funds, or mutual funds. Another recommendation is appreciated assets, that is, assets that have gone up in value. Gain from the sale of the property will be taxed at your child's lower rate, even though the value increased while you were the owner.

Another advantage of a custodian account is that the gift is a transfer from your estate to your child's, thus reducing eventual estate taxes.

Furthermore, a custodian account may provide the best investment choice for minor children who lack the maturity or legal capacity to manage and dispose of certain types of property. For example, you probably wouldn't want to put title to and control of an apartment building in your minor child's name—even if your state permits it. Hiring a fiduciary is costly, and if you keep control and management yourselves, you risk being liable for the taxes.

What are the shortcomings? Once you have given money or other assets to your child under UGMA or UTMA, it is no longer yours. If you unexpectedly need money later, you will have to borrow it from strangers, not your child.

You also have no control over how your child will spend the money when the custodianship ends. Will your child be able to handle the responsibility of suddenly coming into $50,000 to $100,000 at the age of 18 or 21? He could use the fund for college or the ultimate driving machine. If you don't want little Monica to touch the money before she's wearing sensible shoes, you need a regular trust (see below).

Transfers of property under UGMA and UTMA are true gifts and may be subject to gift tax if they exceed $10,000 per year ($20,000 if your spouse joins in).

CHILDREN'S TRUSTS

Trust. The word conjures up blue blood and old money, a legal web spun by the wealthy to coddle wastrels, thwart the grave, and foil the IRS. Certainly, many legal fortunes have been made drawing up trusts named after rich clients.

Despite the multimillion-dollar company it keeps, a trust can be a useful tool for anyone who wants to set property aside for future distribution. The most common uses—to cut estate taxes and to avoid probate—are discussed in Chapter 10. But a trust is another device for shifting income to your lower-bracket child. And it is an effective way to shift income to children who are too young or too inexperienced to manage complex or valuable assets.

A trust is also the recommended way to transfer real estate to children. One reason is that, although a child can receive title to property in most states, he cannot convey it. To sell real estate, a minor child must be represented by a guardian. This leads to court, with all the attendant delay and expense.

Not that setting up even a simple trust is cheap. You can't get by with a do-it-yourself kit. Sure, it's a lot of boilerplate, but only a skilled trust and tax attorney knows *which* boilerplate will meet your desires and goals—and conform to federal and your state laws at the same time. Moreover, you must file annual trust tax returns—an added cost. For these reasons, the cost of a trust outweighs the benefits unless a substantial amount of money or other assets is at stake—at least $50,000.

How does a trust work? In principle, it's like an escrow account. The trust instrument drawn up by your lawyer creates the trust. Hand out cigars because it's a legal person (or entity). Title to the property you want to give is transferred to the trust. The trust is now the legal owner.

You are the **grantor** (or **trustor**). The person you name to oversee the trust and to manage its assets is the **trustee.** Your child is the **beneficiary,** the person who will benefit from the trust. The property held by the trust is called its **principal.**

The life span of the trust is up to you. It can last 5, 15, even 50 years. Some trusts, like the minor's trust described below, expire when a beneficiary reaches a certain age.

Most parents use one of two types of trusts to make gifts to children—a minor's trust or a Crummey trust.

In a **minor's, or 2503(c), trust,** the trustee (normally you) controls the income and principal until your child reaches age 21. At that time, your child has 30 to 60 days to demand the assets. If he fails to do so, the principal remains in trust for a specified time, while the income is distributed annually to your child. The tax appeal is that the first $5,000 earned by the trust is taxed at 15%, regardless of your child's age. Amounts above $5,000 are taxed at 28%.

A **Crummey trust** provides the same tax benefits, but is a lot more tightfisted. The trust principal belongs to your child when he reaches age 21, but he can't take the money and run. Instead, he can withdraw a limited amount each year. The trustee remains in control of the trust until he decides to dissolve it.

You will probably want to act as trustees and to manage the trust yourselves. You must, however, surrender all power over the trust property except for

- the power to distribute income or principal to a qualified charitable organization;
- the power to withhold income temporarily from your child;
- the power to withhold income from your child who is legally disabled or under the age of 21;

- the power to allocate income and expenses between the trust and its income (that is, to attribute some or all of the income and expenses to the trust or some or all of the income and expenses to the income it earns or a little to both);
- the power to use trust income for the support of your child.

In other words, the property is no longer yours. If you act like it is, the income from the trust will be taxed to you. This includes receiving trust income or using it to pay (1) life insurance premiums on your or your spouse's life, (2) your or your spouse's debts, or (3) gift tax on a gift to the trust. You will also be taxed on trust income if you or your spouse (1) have the power to revoke the trust; (2) have the right to receive trust income; or (3) control beneficial enjoyment of the trust—for example, you place your house in trust, but retain the right to live in it without paying rent.

The income of the trust may be distributed to your child as it is earned or when the trust terminates. If income is distributed, it is taxed to your child. For tax reasons, you may want to let income accumulate in the trust until your child reaches 14. Let the trust pay the tax instead at its lower rate.

As trustee, you may spend all of the trust income and principal for your child's welfare before he reaches 21. But you will then be taxed to the extent that that income is used to discharge your legal obligation to provide support.

One of the most common uses of a minor's trust is to finance a child's education. If this is your purpose, make sure that under your state law the legal obligation of support does not include a duty to provide a college education. One way to avoid this problem would be to instruct the trustee to distribute income from the trust directly to your child before or while he's in college. Then cross your fingers that the path to the registrar's office doesn't lead past too many stereo stores.

Similarly, if trust income is used to fulfill a contractual obligation you have made, you will be taxed on that income even if you don't put it to that actual use. If you plan to use the trust to finance your child's education, therefore, you shouldn't contract with the college to pay tuition and other expenses.

If, heaven forbid, your child dies before reaching 21, the undistributed income and principal must be paid to your child's estate.

What property should you place in trust? Ideally, you should transfer property that yields a high rate of return, to profit from the trust's lower tax rate. Try not to transfer encumbered assets. Real estate free of all mortgages and capable of generating a good cash flow is an example of choice trust property. One asset you should not place in trust is life insurance on either yourself or your spouse—the trust income will be taxed to you.

Short-term, or Clifford, trusts. Tax planning did have a Golden Age. In the glory days before tax reform, you could give property away in trust and have it come back to you in a few years like a boomerang. A short-term trust was strictly temporary (at least 10 years and a day). But while it lasted, all income was taxed at your child's lower rate. You had your assets and your tax savings, too.

At the end of the trust period, the principal reverted to you. If you timed it right, the trust ended when your child entered college.

This was too much of a good thing. Congress cornered short-term trusts in a dark alley and clubbed them with tax reform. The blow was nearly fatal: income from short-term trusts is now taxed to the grantor. That's you, the parent.

This means that the trust income is never taxed to your child at his rate, regardless of age.

There are two exceptions. Trust income will be taxed at the beneficiary's lower rate if (1) the trust reverts only after the death of the income beneficiary, who is the grantor's lineal descendant or (2) the value of the grantor's reversionary interest (his right to future enjoyment of the property) when the trust is created does not exceed 5% of the fair market value of the assets placed in trust. This second exception can be met by giving your child an income interest for a term of at least 31.5 years. For example, you give your daughter the right to the income from your rental property for the next 35 years, with the property to come back to you if she dies before you do. The income from the trust will be taxed at your daughter's rate.

SPLIT-INTEREST PURCHASES

You can't point to many things that date back to William the Conqueror. But if you want to step back into the Middle Ages, try property law. Try a split-interest purchase. It's a perfectly modern transaction, based on concepts that seemed old hat to Robin Hood—estates.

Not estates like Blenheim. In law, an estate is your interest in property. This does not necessarily mean complete ownership. Remember, lawyers have mined this ground ceaselessly for centuries. As a result, estates can be shaved, sliced, and parceled out with surgical precision. Estates can be carved up in time, space, and use. You can, for example, sell the rights to cross your property, to see the ocean on a clear day, to drill for oil, even to build a bridge overhead.

In a split-interest purchase, you and your child are dividing up a single estate in time. You buy the right to use and enjoy the property and any income it produces during your life, what's known as a **life estate.** Your child buys the **remainder,** that is, the right to use the same property after you die.

You and your child each pay your proportional share of the cost of the property, based on actuarial tables found in Treasury regulations. This valuation method may not be appropriate, however, if the asset does not produce income (for example, raw land or stock that does not pay dividends). The result could be a determination by the IRS that you have made a taxable gift to your child.

Your child cannot buy his share with money that comes from you. Gifts from grandparents or other relatives can be used, as can wages that your child has earned. If your child has no funds, consider a grantor retained income trust, or GRIT. You keep the income interest, as with a split-purchase, but you put up the entire purchase price. Count on stiff legal fees, however.

The cost of the remainder interest can be reduced if both you and your spouse buy life estates in the property. Your child still receives the same property—he must simply wait longer. Structuring the purchase of income-producing property as a joint and survivor life estate also ensures that the surviving spouse will have a reliable source of income.

What are the attractions of this elaborate scheme? For one thing, you are assured of a steady flow of income during your life. This can be important if you are using other estate-planning techniques to transfer other income-producing property to your children (and grandchildren). Your needs will be taken care of after all your gifts have been made.

Perhaps the greatest advantage is that your child will receive the property tax-free, for a fraction of its cost. This is true even if the property has risen tremendously in value. Your child receives the benefit of the appreciation without having to pay any transfer tax.

Furthermore, a split-interest purchase avoids probate. When you die, the property automatically passes to your child. Title to the remainder interest is transferred to your child when you jointly buy the property, not at your death.

A split-interest purchase also serves to reduce your eventual estate tax, if any. The amount you pay the seller for your life estate comes out of your taxable gross estate. True, you will receive income to replace the purchase price. But if you don't outlive your life expectancy or if you spend all the income, the decrease will be permanent.

Of course there are income tax aspects. You will be taxed on all the income produced by the property. You may not claim depreciation to offset this income when your child owns the remainder interest. On the plus side, your child's basis in the property is increased by the amount of this unallowed depreciation. This will reduce your child's taxable capital gain when the property is sold.

YOUR CHILD'S MONETARY RIGHTS

Does your child have the right to spend or manage his own earnings or other money? Only if you give him that right, either by formal agreement or practice.

Can you touch your child's earnings? Yes, if you are providing his support. The amount you can take is regulated in many states. For example, most of us are familiar with the famous Coogan law, requiring that a percentage of a child performer's wages be placed in trust for him until he reaches the age of majority. If your child is living away from home

or is married, however, you have no rights to his earnings.
Your duty to support your child doesn't end because he
is earning enough to support himself. Not even if he can buy
and sell you. He is entitled to support from you until he
reaches the age of majority or becomes emancipated. Support includes the necessities of life—food, shelter, clothing,
medical care, and education through high school. In some
states, a college education is considered an item of support
in certain circumstances.

Assets your child receives through inheritance or gift may
not be claimed by anyone but your child and then only in
accordance with the terms of the will or gift.

Banking Rights

Your child is not confined to piggy banking. He may open
a bank account in his own name and deposit or withdraw
money. He does not need your consent.

Nonetheless, your child may not withdraw money from a
custodian account set up on his behalf. These funds are in
trust and may be spent only by the trustee.

Wills and Inheritances

You really do have to be of sound mind and body to make
a will. And in the eyes of the state, a minor child does not
have the mental capacity to decide how his assets should be
distributed at death. There is no point to rounding up wit-
nesses, therefore, until your child reaches the age of majority
and can make a valid will. This age varies from state to state.

If your child dies, his property usually goes to you as his
parents. If you both predecease your child, his brothers and
sisters will inherit if he dies. In the absence of siblings, each
state has its own rules, aimed at passing the property to the

closest relatives. If your child is married, the property will go to his spouse and children.

A child does have the right to inherit. Property that you leave to your child will be managed by the guardian or trustee that you appoint in your will until your child comes of age. If there is no will, a court will usually appoint a guardian.

THE WORKING CHILD

That tiny hand curled round your thumb will someday grip a paycheck. Your child's right to work may be restricted, however. The state sees itself as a father figure, and each has rules to protect minors from dangerous and unhealthy jobs, such as operating certain machinery or working near dangerous substances. Age limits may also apply. For example, in California, no child under age 10 can sell or distribute newspapers in urban areas.

The state also regulates your child's work hours: children may not be allowed, for instance, to work before 5:00 A.M. or after 10:00 P.M. or to put in more than 48 hours a week.

Generally, the state does not interfere with children performing work typically done by minors, such as baby-sitting, working in fast-food restaurants, packing groceries, entertaining, or clerking in stores.

Some states require your child to have working papers. Check with your state employment or human resources office for information.

Hiring Your Child

One of the best substitutes for an allowance is to put your child on your payroll. Because the salary is deductible as a business expense, you not only succeed in having a portion of your earnings taxed at a lower rate, you also reduce your net profit subject to self-employment tax.

Furthermore, a dependent child can earn up to $3,400 (indexed for inflation) a year and pay no federal tax. From a tax standpoint, therefore, it is better to pay a child wages than to give him an income-producing gift. Any unearned income over $550 is taxed.

Not only that, but wages paid to a child under the age of 18 are exempt from employment taxes, such as FICA (social security) and unemployment tax. The effective cost of employing your minor child rather than a non-family member is, therefore, much less.

Another nice touch is that paying your minor child a salary does not cost you his exemption—as long as you continue to furnish over half of his support and he is under age 19 or a full-time student under the age of 24.

A word of warning, however. The salary must be reasonable for the type of services rendered. The work must also be bona fide: jobs that you would pay a third person to do if you were not hiring your child. *Note:* Your child must be old enough to perform the assigned work competently. Don't expect the IRS to believe that your five-year-old does your bookkeeping. Making telephone calls, stocking shelves, and taking inventory are genuine tasks suitable to the level of responsibility of a minor child. If these two tests are not met, the salary deduction will not be allowed, and the payments will be treated as gifts.

You should also keep careful time records to prove that your child is a deductible employee. Keep time cards for each child, tracking actual hours spent working and the jobs performed. Pay the salary by check, and make sure that your child deposits the money in an account in his name. Don't name yourself as a trustee of the account, because that indicates that the salary is a gift.

Because your child has earned his paycheck, you can't place restrictions on how the money is spent. He can pay his own school tuition, buy school supplies, purchase a car. Or he can spend it all on rock concerts. Anything except food and shelter, which you are legally required to provide. If that sounds undesirable, consider this: You would probably give your child the money anyway. At least now it is tax-deductible.

Fringe Benefits

Your child is entitled to the same fringe benefits provided to similarly employed adults. Your child may also collect worker's compensation if he is injured on the job or unemployment compensation if he is laid off. And his earnings count toward his eventual social security benefits.

Withholding on Wages

Here's your chance to assume the mantle of wisdom and even drag out a horror story or two. You know all about filling out the Form W-4, *Employee's Withholding Allowance Certificate,* of course. But this is your child's first brush with the IRS. Think how impressed he'll be when you tell him exactly how many withholding allowances he should claim.

Relax. Your child's finances are probably elementary. If so, there are only two choices: (1) to claim "single" with one allowance or (2) to ask to be exempt from withholding.

Naturally, no withholding would be better. Your child will not have to wait for a refund of taxes he does not owe. Not every child qualifies, though. The exemption from withholding is available only if (1) your child had no income tax liability last year and (2) he expects none again this year. But your child *cannot* be exempt if he is another person's dependent, has any non-wage income, and expects to earn more than $550 during the year.

If your child does not qualify for the exemption, he may claim one allowance for his standard deduction if he has wages of at least $2,150 and one for each $2,150 of itemized deductions. *Subtract* one allowance for each $2,150 of non-wage income. *Note:* The $2,150 figure is indexed for inflation, that is, it usually increases each year.

IRA Deduction

You're never too young to start saving for retirement, especially if it saves taxes. Even a child may contribute up to $2,000 of wages to an Individual Retirement Arrangement (IRA). This means that your child's earnings may be set aside in a qualified retirement plan and not be taxed. Or if it seems a bit early to be thinking about your child's retirement, a smaller portion of his wages may be put aside.

YOUR CHILD'S TAX RETURN

Your child must file a tax return if he has unearned income of more than $550 or total gross income in excess of the current standard deduction. He must also file if he has self-employment income of $400 or more.

Of course, you will want to file a return for your child, required or not, in order to claim a refund of any withholding on wages.

Your child is allowed a standard deduction equal to the greater of $550 (indexed for inflation) or his earned income (up to the regular standard deduction). Your child can also itemize if his deductions directly connected with the production of income exceed the standard deduction. Expenses that are directly connected include custodian fees and service charges, fees to collect interest and dividends, and investment counseling fees. These expenses are deductible to the extent they exceed 2% of your child's adjusted gross income.

The standard deduction (or directly connected itemized deductions) reduces unearned income first. The remainder is subtracted from earned income. Itemized deductions that aren't directly connected with producing unearned income can be used to offset the amount of unearned income taxed at your top rate.

No personal exemption may be claimed on your child's return if he is your dependent. This is true even if you do not claim him as an exemption. What matters is that you could have done so.

Let's look at an example. Take Jamie, a professional dancer at age 11, for instance. Jamie earned $4,200 last year. She also received interest income of $1,400. Her itemized deductions for tutus and tap shoes totaled $880. Jamie's taxable income is computed as follows:

Adjusted gross income	$5,600
Less: Larger of itemized deductions, standard deduction ($550), or earned income	4,200
Taxable income	$1,400

Special Rules for Unearned Income

How your child's unearned income is taxed depends solely upon his age. Until he reaches his tax majority at age 14, his unearned income in excess of $1,100 is taxed at *your* top rate. Once your child turns 14, all unearned income is taxed at his lower rate.

Unearned income is income other than compensation for services and includes interest, dividends, rents, royalties, capital gains, and nontaxable scholarships.

The source of unearned income makes no difference. Gifts by grandparents or friends, even earnings on your child's own wages, are still taxed at your highest marginal rate.

Wages that your child **earns** are always taxed at his rate, regardless of age.

Computing the Tax for a Child under 14

Your child's **net unearned income** is taxed in three stages:

1. From $0 to $550—$0 tax*
2. From $551 to $1,100—child's tax rate
3. Over $1,100—parent's top rate

Thus, your child's net unearned investment income over $1,100 is treated as if received by you. Although your child files his own return, his tax rate is based on your Form 1040.

For purposes of this rule, *net* unearned income equals your child's unearned income minus the larger of (1) $1,100 or (2) the $550 standard deduction plus his itemized deductions, if any.

For example, Robin, age 10, has $1,800 of interest income on a custodian account. She also has $600 of earned income, with $750 of itemized deductions. Robin's taxable income is:

* Figures are indexed for inflation.

Total income	$2,400
Less: Larger of itemized deductions, standard deduction ($550), or earned income	750
Taxable income	$1,650

Robin's income subject to tax at her parents' top rate is:

Unearned income	$1,800
Less: Larger of (1) $1,100 or (2) standard deduction ($550) plus itemized deductions ($750)	1,300
Net unearned income taxed at parents' rate	$ 500

The amount of tax your child pays is the difference between (1) the tax you would have paid if your child's unearned income were included on your own return and (2) the tax you are actually paying. Use Form 8615 to calculate your child's tax.

A special election allows you to report your child's gross income over $1,000 on your own return. Use Form 8814 to make this election. You must pay an additional tax equal to the lesser of $75 or 15% of your child's income over $500.

For instance, Bart and Julie have an 8-year-old daughter, Annie. Last year, Annie received $1,300 in dividends, but no other income. No estimated tax payments were made in her name. Bart and Julie elect to include Annie's dividends on their Form 1040, instead of filing a return for her. They include $300 of the dividends on the "Other income" line of the Form 1040 ($1,300 − $1,000). They also add $75 to their tax, because it is lower than 15% of Annie's income in excess of $500 ($1,300 − $500 = $800 × 15% = $120).

Should you make the election? You'll have less paperwork, but the tax will be about the same. Reporting your child's income as your own, however, makes it harder to deduct medical expenses and miscellaneous itemized deductions, which are reduced by a percentage of your adjusted gross income. On the other hand, including your child's income may allow you to deduct more investment interest. This deduction can't exceed your investment income.

What if you and your spouse are filing separate returns? Your child's tax is computed based upon the income of the spouse with the higher taxable income.

If you have more than one child under 14 with unearned income, lay in a supply of adding machine tape. Your children's unearned incomes are combined, and the tax you would pay on the total is computed. You must then prorate each child's share of your additional tax, based on the ratio of each child's income to the total unearned income of all your children.

Take Sam and Darlene, for example. They are the tax-happy parents of Ricky, age 9, and Brian, age 6. The custodian accounts, started when each child was in the cradle, earned $1,400 for Ricky and $1,200 for Brian last year. Ricky's share of his parents' tax will be 54% ($1,400/$2,600) and Brian's will be 46% ($1,200/$2,600).

Estimated Tax

Because there is no withholding on unearned income, your child may be required to make estimated tax payments. Estimated tax must be paid if the total tax liability will be $500 or more and the total amount of withholding will be less than the *smaller* of: (1) 90% of your child's expected income tax or (2) 100% of his last year's tax.

Unless your child is working and can adjust his withholding, make sure the estimated tax payment is paid each quarter. Use Form 1040-ES. *Note:* State estimated tax may also be due.

Liability for Your Child's Tax

Who is liable if your child does not pay his income tax? Under state law, a child's wages belong to the parent, and thus you are liable for tax on those earnings. You are not accountable for income tax on unearned income, such as interest or dividends, however.

SOCIAL SECURITY NUMBER FOR YOUR CHILD

While you are out stocking up on Pampers, be sure to stop at the Social Security Administration. The social security number of every dependent who is at least *two* years old must be reported on your tax return.

To obtain a number, ask your local social security office for Form SS-5. You will need your child's original birth certificate or a certified copy. You can apply for the number by mail.

9

PAYING AS THEY GROW: Your Child's College Education

We've all heard the horror stories. How financing a college education is like buying a 747 on layaway. How alma mater has become "Mommie Dearest." How the cost of a Harvard B.A. will be $154,200 by the year 2000.

It's true. A cap and gown in the twenty-first century will cost more than $90,000 at a private college ($50,000 at a state university). This numbing figure could be viewed dispassionately if simple inflation were the culprit. Your income would rise by an equally lofty amount. But college costs have outstripped inflation since 1980. The real cost of attending a private university shot up 26% between 1980 and 1985, compared with a 7.5% rise in real personal income. And there is no relief in sight. Tuition is expected to leap 7% a year for the next decade. In fact, scholars have recently discovered that the word "campus" comes from an old Latin word meaning "an arm and a leg."

With anything else this catastrophic—cancer, court-

204 | SPROUSE'S TWO-EARNER MONEY BOOK

awarded damages, Chernobyl—you could buy insurance. As it is, you are on your own. The familiar resources—government grants and loans—are drying up. You won't get any help from the tax man, either. Tax reform has actually increased the cost of college by taking a bigger bite out of your college fund.

You must be self-reliant. With two incomes, you should not count entirely on financial aid. You will probably have to shoulder a large share of college expenses yourselves. That means planning is paramount. Don't freeze in the glare of the six-digit wipeout hurtling at you. Bold and creative action is needed. The task ahead is too overwhelming to rely on modest savings kept in low-interest bank accounts. Yet 42% of parents do just that.

There is a bright side. Despite shocking headlines, quality education is still available for half the Ivy League cost, particularly at public colleges. If you don't insist on a "name" school, your child can receive an excellent education at relatively bargain prices.

Financial aid will not be extinct, either. Even with an income as high as $75,000, you may be able to qualify if you have three or more children in college. Still, aid is much more likely to be in the form of loans than outright grants. You will probably have to come up with most of the cash, but at least you or your child will be able to spread some of the costs over several years.

This chapter explores the strategies and investments that enable you to accumulate the cash you will need, no matter what age your child is when you first begin saving. We'll analyze some of the innovative financial products being introduced to allay fears that college will soon be beyond most people's reach. And we'll take a look at sources of financial aid and their eligibility requirements.

COMPUTING COLLEGE COSTS

It's not enough to save—you must also save enough. And no investment plan can hit the mark unless you pinpoint the target. This means estimating your child's college costs and calculating how much you must lay away between now and the freshman year.

This is by no means easy. Your fund must anticipate the future. What college will your child attend? How high will the tuition be? Will your child go on to graduate studies, or worse, medical school? How much and what type of financial aid will be available? And a host of other unknowns.

Warm up your computer if you have one. Juggling hypothetical numbers is what computers do best. Then go fact-finding. Pick four or five schools that your child is likely to attend, and write or call the admissions office of each to find out the current costs for four years. Don't stop with tuition. Ask about room and board, books, supplies, and fees charged in addition to tuition, such as student activity fees. Add in transportation, health care, and personal expenses (pizza, movies, telephone).

Now assume an inflation rate of 7% a year. Multiply the current cost times 7% times the number of years before your child enters college. Add this figure to the current cost. For example, if a B.A. at Bankrupt U currently sets you back $50,000 and your child is 10 years away from admission, you will need to save $85,000 ($50,000 × 7% × 10 years plus $50,000 current cost).

After you recover from the shock, compute how much money you must set aside each year, assuming a realistic rate of return, for example, 8% a year. Don't forget taxes. Taxes evaporate savings. The rate of evaporation is your top bracket, say 31%. You must, therefore, add 31% to your targeted amount. In our example, you would have to save $111,350 to net $85,000 after taxes ($85,000 × 131%).

What's the bottom line? If your child is still in diapers, you will have to salt away between $1,500 and $4,000 a year to cover future college costs. If you get a late start, the annual savings required rises steeply. For every five years later that you begin, you should approximately double the amount you invest.

Note: The above figures presume you will ante up the full cost yourselves. Loans, scholarships, and summer jobs may ease the strain. For that reason, save all you reasonably can without being obsessive to the point of hardship.

INVESTING FOR COLLEGE

Before you start a bank account or plunge into mutual funds, you should decide who will own the funds. In some cases, tax savings can be realized by putting investments in your child's name. This is usually done by opening a custodian account or by setting up a minor's trust.

The theory behind this strategy, known as income shifting, is that your child will be in a lower tax bracket than you. And every dollar snatched from the tax man is one less dollar you have to save.

Unfortunately, if your child is under age 14, investment income of over $1,100 is taxed at *your* top rate. For this reason, if your child is under 14, go with investments that defer earnings. When your child turns 14, shift to funds that yield high current income.

You can also time your gifts, giving as little as possible when your child is young, then stepping up gift giving about the time your child reaches 14. For example, if you have targeted $100,000 to put your infant through college, you can make an initial gift of $15,000 at birth. Let this money compound virtually tax-free until your child turns 13. Then contribute $20,000 at ages 13 and 14. This will achieve your goal and save over $9,000 in taxes.

One argument against income shifting is that it will reduce the amount of any financial aid. Colleges expect students to use 35% of any assets in their own names toward school, but only 5.6% of assets in the parents' names.

For a complete discussion of income shifting and your child's taxes, see Chapter 8.

Once you have settled on whose name to invest in, you can map out an investment plan. Besides tax planning, your choice of investments will depend upon how long you have before your child will take the campus by storm. The strategies set forth below, therefore, suggest the best ways to invest your savings at different stages in your child's life.

Cradle to Kindergarten

Start saving before your child is in grade school, and you have an asset money can't buy—time. Not only do you have more time to put money aside, but those dollars have time to compound. Compounding is money's magic act. You have only to set aside $1,000 at 8% today to have $4,200 in 18 years. Time kicks in $3,200. Sock away $1,000 each year and your $18,000 investment turns into $37,450.

If you want to send your newborn to a private college (let's assume an average annual cost of $12,000), you would need to set aside about $300 a month for one year's expenses. Wait until age 9 and you have to scrape up about $450 each month. And if you don't start until your child has 15 candles on his cake, it will take almost $800 a month to meet your goal.

Just because you have time doesn't mean you should let it do all the work. Think in terms of investing, not merely saving. Time allows you to be more aggressive, to make up any losses on higher-risk investments. There's another reason for being less conservative. Time has a downside—inflation. Low-yielding investments may not be able to weather its erosive effects for 13 to 18 years. You should, therefore, invest some of your money for higher returns than you can receive from such traditional college-savings vehicles as U.S. savings bonds.

Growth stock mutual funds. These funds invest in stocks of companies with growth potential. They pay little or no current dividends, thereby avoiding the kiddie tax, but are expected to appreciate in value. These are riskier than other mutual funds, but they have the best long-term performance. That's perfect, because you are going to hold them for at least 10 years.

Select a fund based on its total return, not its yield. Yield measures only the amount of income paid to investors. Total return takes into account fluctuations in the fund's share price as well. Stock mutual fund prices are not constant, but vary with bond prices. A mutual fund could, therefore, lose more in value than it is paying in yield, leaving you with a net loss.

Avoid load funds and funds that charge more than 1% a year in administrative, advisory, or "12b-1" fees. Studies have shown that no-load funds perform as well, on average, as load funds that usually charge an 8.5% sales commission. The $850 you will save on every $10,000 you invest can go toward building your college fund.

Stay away from funds that charge surrender fees to withdraw your money. A mutual fund is supposed to be liquid. And sidestep sector funds that invest in gold or particular industries unless you believe you have the expertise to out-guess a good diversified mutual fund manager.

Once you have narrowed down your choices, call each fund's toll-free number for a prospectus. Choose a fund that has performed well in both good and bad markets. Examine track records for at least five years. This information is also published in *Forbes, Barron's,* and *Money.* Compare the services that each fund provides, too, including the ability to switch money among a family of funds.

You can buy into most funds for an initial investment of $1,000. Some have no minimum at all. Thus, you don't have to put all of your money into one fund. Don't choose so many funds that you get bogged down in record keeping, however.

Zero-coupon bonds. These innovative investment vehicles let you lay out a relatively modest sum today and receive an impressive amount at a specific date in the future. And you know in advance exactly how much you'll come into when the bond reaches maturity. What easier way to meet your goal than four zero-coupon bonds timed to mature during each of your child's college years?

Another virtue of zero-coupon bonds is that they require no management. You make a one-time purchase and lock them away in a safe place for 10 to 20 years. Ideal for a busy parent.

Zero-coupon bonds pay no current interest. You buy the bonds at a substantial discount from the $1,000 face value. For example, a zero-coupon bond yielding 9% that matures in 10 years might cost $390, compared with its $1,000 face value. When the bond matures, you collect the full $1,000.

The $610 difference between your cost and the face value is, in effect, accumulated interest.

You must pay tax on the interest as it accrues each year, even though you won't see the money for years. This makes zeros a good investment for a custodian account. If your child has no other income, he will pay little or no tax on the interest. Or you can avoid tax on this "phantom interest" by buying zero-coupon municipal bonds, issued by states and municipalities. These are exempt from federal tax and if you are a resident of the issuing state, from state and local taxes as well.

Make sure you won't need the money before the bond's maturity. The prices of long-term zeros are far more volatile than ordinary bonds. If you are forced to sell at the wrong moment, you could suffer a jarring loss.

Be wary of bonds that are **callable.** This means they can be redeemed by the issuer before they mature. Once you have locked in a good interest rate for the right length of time, you want to hold on to the bond till maturity. You don't want to go searching for a new investment that may not have as high a yield. Check the prospectus to see if the bond is callable according to an "accretion schedule."

Safety should be a prime concern. You are banking on the distant future. You can't collect your $1,000 if the issuer has long since gone bankrupt. Your best bet is zero-coupon Treasury bonds (sometimes known as TIGRs, CATS, and STRIPS) or federally insured zero certificates of deposit. Less than 100% safe are zeros issued by corporations and municipalities and those backed by mortgages. Avoid zero-coupon unit trusts or bond funds because they charge high sales fees and often invest in riskier zero-coupon corporate "junk" bonds.

A new form of tax-free zero, issued in some states, is **college savings bonds,** or **baccalaureate bonds.** As of early

1989, nine states were selling these bonds, and eight others had announced plans to do so. College savings bonds generally have two advantages over other municipal zeros: they have higher credit ratings and are not callable.

Zeros are subject to spreads of up to 10%, so it pays to shop around when you are both buying and selling. The yield on a bond reflects the broker's fee. Make sure the broker doesn't plan to add on an extra commission after computing the yield.

Tuition prepayment plans. Want to get a jump on the twenty-first century? Don't wait for your child to enter college. Pay the full four years' tuition now—at a substantial discount. No more fears about price hikes and inflation. Instant peace of mind.

Right now three states—Florida, Michigan, and Wyoming—have such prepayment plans. Five others—Alabama, Indiana, Missouri, Oklahoma, and West Virginia—have them in the works. In addition, about fifteen private colleges have also set up some form of prepayment plan.

Also known as **endowed tuition plans** and **tuition futures,** these devices allow you to pay anywhere from a few months to 18 years in advance. The money is usually paid in one lump sum, although installment payments are sometimes possible. The younger your child, the lower the cost. If your child is quite young, the cost could be as low as the cost of one year's tuition at the current rate.

Quite a bargain. Or is it? In practice, these plans have serious drawbacks. For one thing, your money is not earning interest. If you want or need your money back, your prepayment will be returned to you, but you will have lost the income that money could have earned if it had been invested normally.

And what if your child doesn't want to go to Prepaid U?

What if it doesn't offer naval architecture or forestry or a film school? What if its top-ten ranking for academic excellence plummets by the year 2007? What if your child won't qualify for admission? Unless your child attends the college you've invested in, you forfeit the interest you could have earned on the money. Worse, if he doesn't complete the first year, you lose every penny. (At most schools, your child may transfer all the money after attending one full year.)

Statewide plans at least increase the odds that your child will benefit from your foresight by allowing attendance at any public university or community college within the state. Generally, your child must be a state resident to participate.

There is no guarantee that Prepaid U won't go under, either, taking your money with it. And finally, prepayment reduces or eliminates outright your child's chances of receiving financial aid—a concern for middle-class families.

Ultimately, prepayment plans involve too much risk. You will do far better to put that same bundle of money into a high-yield investment, like a growth stock mutual fund, where it will be liquid and earning income.

If you are still dazzled by the potential savings of prepayment, at least research all of your options carefully. Ask these questions: (1) Does it cover all college costs, or only tuition? (2) Is the plan's yield guaranteed? (3) Can your investment be transferred to another family member? (4) What are the residency requirements? (5) Is the plan insured? (6) Can funds be withdrawn early in the event of an emergency, and will any interest be paid on your investment?

Before you invest in a prepayment plan, you should also know the **tax consequences.** According to a 1988 IRS ruling on the Michigan plan, your child will be taxed on the future benefit, but not until he attends college. The amount taxed is the tuition the plan pays minus your initial investment. This difference, which represents the income that your initial investment has earned while it has been in the state's keeping all these years, is spread over each of the four years that your child is in college. For example, if you put up $8,000 that covers four years of tuition worth $20,000, your child would pay federal tax at his rate on $3,000 income in each of those four years ($20,000/4 − $8,000/4).

Note: Variations in state plans may cause the IRS to tax other plans differently, although this has not yet happened.

That's not all. Your up-front payment is considered a taxable gift. The $10,000 exclusion ($20,000 for married couples acting jointly) from gift tax does not apply, because the gift's value lies in the future. The lifetime estate and gift tax credit, however, will shelter most payments from tax. Declare the amount of tax you owe on Form 709, subtracting it from the $192,800 unified estate and gift tax credit allowed when you die.

Ages 6 to 11

Your goal during these years should be to diversify with more conservative investments than during infancy. Growth is still more desirable than current income, because of the kiddie tax, but avoid a high level of risk.

Total return mutual funds and utility stocks. You can strike a balance between growth and income by choosing a **total return mutual fund.** These funds invest in a mix of growth stocks, high-dividend stocks, and bonds. Their aim is to provide a steady return from a combination of capital gains and interest or dividends. This makes their prices more stable than a growth fund, but also can make long-term performance less spectacular.

Total return funds should be held at least five years. As with growth stock mutual funds discussed above, avoid load funds and funds that charge more than 1% in administrative or marketing fees.

Select a fund that contains more common stocks than bonds. They are more growth-oriented than funds that focus on bonds.

Consider funds that are part of a fund family. These offer a variety of funds and allow you to switch between them. This will be a valuable feature when your child reaches age 14, and you begin to move savings into fixed-income investments, such as money market and income mutual funds.

If you have the time and experience, you may want to invest part of your savings in individual stocks. Remember, however, that, unlike a mutual fund, you are entrusting your eggs pretty much to one basket. Low risk is, therefore, a top priority. The prices of **utility stocks** have historically been stable. Although you sacrifice growth, you gain excellent income. Such companies reinvest only a small percentage of their earnings, paying out the rest as dividends. Better still, due to paper losses from tax write-offs, some utilities pay dividends that are a nontaxable return of capital.

Before selecting a utility, check for companies that have a long, unbroken record of paying dividends. If those dividends have been consistently increasing, so much the better.

Again, be prepared to hold this stock for at least five years.

Series EE savings bonds. Always a popular college-savings device, these U.S. savings bonds now offer a special tax break that's hard to refuse. Beginning in 1990, interest on EE bonds is tax-free if spent on higher education for yourself, your spouse, or your child. Qualified bonds must be issued after 1989 to an individual age 24 or older and must be redeemed in the year that college tuition is paid. Converting the old E or EE bonds you own to new bonds after 1989 will not qualify.

You must buy the bonds yourself in your own or your spouse's name. Bonds purchased as gifts in your child's name won't qualify for the exclusion, nor will bonds purchased by a relative and put in your name.

The exclusion is available only for tuition and fees paid in the year that you redeem the bond. Only tuition and fees in excess of any nontaxable scholarships and employer-provided educational assistance received qualify for the exclusion. Tuition for nursing schools and some vocational schools qualify, but not the cost of any sports education unless it is part of a degree program.

If the total amount of principal and interest redeemed is less than the tuition and fees you paid, all of your savings bond interest will be tax-free. But if the redemption amount is more than your costs, a portion of the interest will be taxed.

Note: This tax break cannot be claimed by higher-income families. The tax-free amount begins to phase out when adjusted gross income in the year that the bonds are redeemed exceeds $60,000 on a joint return, and is no longer available at $90,000 joint. The exclusion cannot be taken if you and your spouse file separate returns.

Even if you won't qualify for the interest exclusion, EE bonds offer other tax breaks that make them a fruitful way to build your college fund. First of all, interest that the bond earns is exempt from state and local taxes, which boosts their after-tax yield. Second, federal tax is not due until the bond is cashed in. Thus, tax can be deferred until your child reaches age 14, when he will be taxed at his lower rate.

Flexible tax planning is possible, though. Your child may elect to report the interest each year instead. This makes sense if your child's total investment income, including the savings bond interest, will be less than $550 a year (with annual wages of less than the standard deduction). In that case, your child won't be required to file a return, and the interest will escape tax completely. Once your child has made this election, he must continue to do so unless the IRS grants permission to change.

Savings bonds are sold by most banks and savings institutions. You may also be able to buy them at work, through a payroll savings plan. They are available in eight denominations, from $50 to $10,000, which you buy for half the face value. For example, a $1,000 bond costs $500.

The term of a bond depends on the interest rate in effect when the bond is issued. The interest rate is guaranteed if you hold the bond for at least five years. After that the interest rate fluctuates, but it will never drop below the guaranteed rate.

Single-premium life insurance. These policies, also called **endowment contracts,** are part life insurance, part savings account. A portion of the single premium you pay goes toward insurance coverage. The balance goes into a savings fund that accumulates cash value. You can borrow from this fund with no obligation to repay. Not only that, the income your investment earns is tax-deferred.

An ideal way to build a college fund, you might say. Especially if you are not a disciplined saver or if you need insurance. When your child is ready for college, you can withdraw up to 90% of the cash value or borrow against it at low or no interest. If you leave enough cash value unborrowed, you can keep the policy in force and never pay back the loan. Or you can make the payments and have an even heftier cash value for retirement. And, if anything should happen to you, your child will receive the death benefit—tax-free.

Sound too good to be true? Then you won't be surprised to learn that Congress recently lowered the boom. Borrow or withdraw cash from your policy, and the amount is taxed first as taxable income to the extent of policy earnings. Worse, loans or withdrawals before age 59½ are subject to a 10% penalty (unless you become disabled or receive payments as an annuity over your expected life).

There are other disadvantages. Up-front commissions are usually steep, which can reduce your yield considerably. Once you buy such a policy, you are more or less forced to keep it because of severe surrender charges. Finally, your rate of return is not guaranteed. The seductive rate that a company may use to lure you into signing can be cut sharply within a year or two. If interest rates rise, your insurer may or may not pass them on to you.

In most cases, a single-premium life policy is a costly and inefficient way to save for college.

Ages 12 to 16

College may be only a dreamlike vision from the cradle, but as elementary school ends, it takes on a distinct, even formidable, shape. The sight jolts many parents into saving for college for the first time.

If you feel like the captain of the *Titanic* just spotting the iceberg, don't panic. You still have time to maneuver. Remember, you won't need all of your savings in the freshman year. A child entering ninth grade has six years before reaching the midpoint of college. You may also be able to borrow some of the cost and to pay another portion out of your cash flow while your child is in college.

Resist the impulse, therefore, to make up for lost time by sinking your money into risky investments, such as individual growth stock and junk bond funds. Any losses this late in the game may be impossible to recoup.

Whether you are just beginning to save or have an enviable

college-savings program already in place, caution is called for. Consider a move into the investments listed below.

Fixed-income investments. This is no time to be standing on shaky ground. You need the firm footing of investments that guarantee 100% of your principal back. You're also in the market for a respectable flow of income. Your child will soon be 14, if he isn't already, when all of his income will be taxed at his own low rate. Your best bets are money market funds and certificates of deposit.

Money market mutual funds are similar to checking accounts that earn interest. They generally pay a higher rate than bank certificates of deposit, and you can withdraw your money at any time without penalty. Although funds are not federally insured, they have an excellent safety record. Income comes from a variety of short-term securities, such as Treasury bills and corporate notes.

The price of money market fund shares remains constant at $1. This means that return of your investment is guaranteed. And the checkwriting privilege gives you immediate access when it comes time to pay those college bills.

Certificates of deposit are accounts with time locks on them. In return for a higher interest rate than a regular passbook account, you agree to leave your money on deposit for a set period, usually six months to five years. Unless the economy is topsy-turvy, the longer you sign up for, the higher the rate of interest.

You can't touch your money early without penalty. That may even be a benefit if you are tempted to raid the cookie jar. Buy CDs timed to mature at the beginning of each fall semester.

Certificates of deposit require a high minimum deposit, commonly from $1,000 to $2,500. If you are just starting your savings program, stick to money markets that allow minimum deposits beginning at $1,000.

Interest earned on CDs exceeding one year is taxed annually, even though you cannot withdraw the income without penalty. Putting the CD in your child's name can reduce the tax bite. But as we discussed above, it can also reduce the amount of financial aid your child eventually receives.

A certificate of deposit is ironically both perfectly safe and risky. The risk is inflation. What if you lock into a five-year deposit at 8%, only to watch college costs soar into double digits? The College Savings Bank of Princeton, New Jersey, has tried to solve this dilemma by inventing the **College-Sure CD.**

On paper it sounds terrific. Instead of tying its interest rate to something as mundane as the prime rate, the bank uses as an index the average annual increases at 500 tony private colleges. The CD thus *guarantees* to cover your child's future tuition and room and board. The cost of your CD is based on the price of your chosen college and your child's present age.

In practice, there are problems that are more than academic. If the College Board index skyrockets, the bank might be hard pressed to pay the guaranteed amounts without making unsound investments that could lead to failure. Furthermore, the bank charges an up-front premium that can shave your yield by about two percentage points below the College Board index. You may wind up earning little more than with a passbook savings account.

If your child is 13, consider a one-year **Treasury bill.** The price is $10,000. No tax is due on the interest until the T-bill is paid on maturity. By that time, your 14-year-old will be taxed at his own lower rate. As a bonus, the interest will be exempt from state and local tax.

Give appreciated stock. If you throw just one birthday party for your child, do so when he turns 14. This is the year the income on college funds in his name is finally taxed at his lower rate. So along with the video games and other presents, why not put a ribbon on that stock you bought years ago when everyone laughed at the idea of car phones?

If you sell the stock to pay for college, your windfall will be taxed at up to 31%. Give the stock to your child who is 14 or older, and let him cash in the shares. The tax will shrink to 15%, less than half what you would pay.

Use the same strategy for the growth stock mutual fund shares you bought when your teenager was still in the crib. Reinvest the sale proceeds in a fixed-income fund.

Note: Shifting assets to your child can minimize future financial aid by making him appear less needy.

401(k) retirement plan. You can sock away up to $8,475 (indexed for inflation) in wages each year through your company's 401(k) plan. You pay no tax on the deferred income or the interest it earns until the money is withdrawn, usually at retirement. Better still, many companies match 25% to 100% of your contribution.

How does this help pay for Freshman English and dorm fees? First, your deferred salary doesn't count as income or assets in assessing your eligibility for financial aid. Second, if your company permits borrowing, you can use your 401(k) funds to pay educational expenses (see "Ages 17 to 18" below).

After-school jobs. All right, there's only so much money to be made by filling tacos and baby-sitting. But you can profit from your child's learning the value of labor and money. Besides, any dollars he saves can relieve you of paying for clothes and personal expenses. And the experience gained can lead to higher-paying jobs in college.

If you own a business, hire your child instead of giving him an allowance. Besides being an excellent method of splitting income, putting your child on the payroll increases your deductible wages. What other strategy lets you finance college and deduct it too?

For a thorough discussion on employing your child, see Chapter 8.

AGES 17 TO 18

As the countdown to college begins, you may feel like a driver on a lonely road at night staring bleakly at an empty gas gauge and wondering how far it is to the next town. Luckily, you can probably get extra mileage from financial aid, borrowing, or one of the creative financing plans offered by more and more schools. If you discover that the distance between your college savings and the amount your child will need is too great, consider the following possibilities:

401(k) loan or IRA withdrawal. Anytime you can get an interest-free loan, you might as well take it. So if your employer's plan permits it, you may want to borrow against the amount in your 401(k) retirement account. You must pay interest—at market rates set by the company's trustees—but the interest payments go into your own account. In effect, free money.

To be eligible, you may have to show you can't raise the money from other sources, such as a bank or an investment. Your employer can take your word for this if you (1) first take all distributions and loans available to you from other plans; (2) agree to make no new contributions to the plan for at least 12 months; and (3) restrict your 401(k) contribution in the following taxable year to the annual limit minus your contribution in the year of the loan.

Generally, these loans must be repaid within five years, with payments of principal and interest every 3 months. Your borrowing is limited to $50,000, reduced by the amount paid on any outstanding loan during the last 12 months.

You cannot *withdraw* money from a 401(k) while you are still working for the company unless you suffer financial hardship. There is no such restriction on **IRA funds.** If your child won't finish college until you or your spouse is age 59½, tapping your IRA accounts may be the way to go. The amount taken out must be included in income on your 1040, but you will dodge the 10% penalty for early withdrawal. Don't forget that you were saving those funds for retirement, however. Think about loaning the money to your child. Then live off the monthly payments in your old age.

Home-equity loan. Are you one of that new elite—the equity-rich? If rocketing real estate prices have made you wealthy on paper, why not cash in on your home's undreamed-of value to invest in a diploma?

What gives home-equity loans the edge over other loans is their deductibility. You can borrow up to $100,000 against your equity, and the interest will be fully deductible. It does not matter how you spend the money—college, cars, or cruises. This means that at a rate of 11%, a home-equity loan actually costs you only 7.59% if you are in the 31% bracket (7.92% in the 28% bracket).

If you have several children headed for college, the $100,000 ceiling on write-offs may be an obstacle. If you borrow more than $100,000 against your home equity, interest on the excess is nondeductible personal interest.

Take out your home-equity loan before applying for any financial aid. The loan reduces your assets and enhances your child's chance of qualifying for aid.

Evaluate your ability to make repayment carefully before borrowing. Miss a couple of payments, and you can lose your home. Financial experts advise against spending more than 25% of your gross income for housing expenses.

Merit scholarships. Susy and Johnny are *your* children, aren't they? That means they're bright, gifted, and more than capable of winning a scholarship based on their academic or athletic ability—not on financial need.

A scholarship is found money. It does not have to be repaid. Naturally, the competition is fierce. But with above-average grades and Scholastic Aptitude Test scores, your talented teenager can reap from $100 to a free ride to college. The same is true if he or she has athletic prowess—and not just in football or basketball. Baseball, tennis, swimming, gymnastics all have their backers. Your child doesn't have to be a Payton or Jabar to qualify either, merely good for his or her age.

There are scholarships aplenty. Nearly 90% of all colleges award merit scholarships. Check with college financial aid officers for information. Don't overlook private scholarships, though. Among these are the prestigious National Merit Scholarship Program, which awards more than $15 million each year, based on academic excellence. Others are given by labor unions, corporate employers, trade associations, civic and fraternal organizations, service clubs (Rotary Club, for example), ethnic organizations, fraternities and sororities, and churches). Some scholarships even go to students who are destined for specific careers.

Start with your child's high school guidance office for help in finding grants from local organizations. Call your state's

Department of Education to find out if they award grants to keep top scholars in-state. Ask the employee benefits department where you work if your company has a scholarship program. If not, suggest starting one.

Tracking down every possible source is obviously time-consuming. This has led to an entire industry offering **computerized scholarship search services.** For around $75, these companies will search several data bases and print a list of all financial aid programs that match your child's profile. These can include not only outright grants, but loans and student work programs. These services rarely provide information on local aid. You will still have to do your own legwork to locate these sources.

Some high school guidance offices offer similar computerized search programs at no cost.

Once your child's genius has been recognized, don't overlook the tax consequences. Scholarships and grants awarded to degree candidates are not taxable to the extent that they are spent on tuition, course-required books, supplies, and equipment. Amounts used for room and board and incidental expenses are *taxable.* If it looks like your child will owe more than $500 tax, he should make estimated tax payments.

Advanced placement. Three years of college are a lot cheaper than four. If your child scores high enough on the advanced placement tests offered by one-third of all high schools, there are more than 1,000 colleges that will let him enter as a sophomore. For more information, write to Advanced Placement Program, Box 300, The College Board, New York, NY 10019.

Payment plans. Soaring costs give colleges anxiety attacks, too. After all, they need a full house. Or at least enough students to fill a football stadium. Don't expect lower prices, however. Like auto manufacturers, more than 700 colleges are experimenting with creative financing. These include low-rate loans with lengthy repayment periods, tuition installment plans, and discounts for prepaying tuition.

A few examples. At the University of Pennsylvania, you can pay all four years in advance at the freshman rate, escaping future tuition increases. The school will even lend you the money at a variable rate 1% above prime to do so. Similar plans are in effect at Case Western Reserve University and Washington University in St. Louis.

At the University of Southern California, you can pay the annual costs over nine monthly installments, starting in the spring. Comparable plans are offered at Stanford University and Pepperdine University in Los Angeles. USC also allows you to pay for all four years up front at a discount, but will not loan you the lump-sum amount.

And many colleges are simply making loans to students at below-market rates.

Even such elite schools as Brown, Harvard, Princeton, and Yale are providing low-rate loans. They are members of the Consortium on Financing Higher Education, a group of 30 Ivy League and other private colleges that hands out annual loans of $2,000 to $15,000. Funds are raised by the nonprofit Nellie Mae (New England Educational Loan Marketing Corporation). You have up to 15 years to repay, at a variable rate that cannot exceed two points above the prime.

Federal aid programs. Despite cutbacks, the U.S. government continues to dwarf other sources of financial aid, providing 75% of the total. Altogether, undergraduates received more than $10 billion in aid in 1988. There has been a shift from gift to debt, however. Today, students must borrow $9 for every $1 they receive in grants (up from a loan-to-grant ratio of $6 to $1). As a result, the number of graduates in debt more than tripled in the past 10 years.

Why should you wade into the quicksand of application forms if you are fairly certain you're too well-off to qualify? Because each college evaluates a family's financial data differently, making allowances for how many children you have, heavy medical costs, other debts, even its own tuition. Let's face it, even a high-income family may need financial aid if Jennifer has her heart set on Harvard. In fact, financial aid officers place roughly the same ceiling on how much you must pay whether your child chooses Sarah Lawrence (annual cost $19,980) or Southern U. and A. & M. ($5,510). If you can afford the full cost at some schools, but not others, apply for assistance only at the most expensive.

All families, regardless of income, are eligible for the government's PLUS loans (see below).

To receive financial aid, you must fill out an application form—either the FAF (Financial Aid Form) or FFS (Family Financial Statement). Get an early start. Applications should be sent to the college in January of your child's senior year of high school. Grab the first appointment on your tax preparer's schedule, too: a copy of your current year's return is expected no later than early February.

Both forms are multipurpose. Each can be used to apply for all federal programs, aid from colleges themselves, and most state aid as well. *Note:* California, Illinois, and Pennsylvania publish their own forms. Ask the college financial aid office or the high school guidance office for the form you need.

The amount of need-based financial aid that a family receives is based on the difference between the cost of attending the school and an estimate of how much you can afford to pay. After adjustment for taxes, financial aid officers expect students to contribute 70% of their income and 35% of their assets each year and parents to chip in as much as 47% of their incomes and 5.6% of their assets. For example, a four-member family, with $60,000 income and $50,000 equity in their home, might have to come up with roughly $10,700 a year to send one child to college. If both children are attending, however, the family's share drops to about half that amount per child. For an advance look at how large a contribution will be expected of you, write for a free pamphlet, *Meeting College Costs* (College Scholarship Service, Box 2843, Princeton, NJ 08541).

The U.S. Department of Education sponsors six aid programs, of which five are based on need. You can get a detailed description of these programs in a free booklet called *The Student Guide: Five Financial Aid Programs* (Federal Student Aid Programs, Department CY-87, Pueblo, CO 81009).

As a rule, **Pell grants** (which do not have to be repaid) go to families with incomes of around $30,000 and below. Awards range from $200 to $2,300 (the maximum varies each year). Students with extreme need may also receive **Supplemental Educational Opportunity Grants (SEOG)**. The maximum SEOG award is usually $4,000 per year.

Perkins loans are made directly by colleges, with 90% of the money provided by the federal government. The interest rate is only 5% with 10 years to repay, starting nine months after graduation. This is the cheapest way to borrow if your child qualifies. Family income must generally be $30,000 or less. The maximum loan amount is $4,500 for the first two years and no more than $9,000 for all four years ($18,000 for graduate students).

Stafford loans are handled by private lenders, such as banks and credit unions. Your child is eligible if he can prove financial need—regardless of your income. The loan amount will depend upon how much extra cash is needed after you make the required family contribution. Students will usually qualify if parental income is less than $65,000, especially if the chosen school is expensive or if more than one child is in college.

The maximum loan is $2,625 a year for freshmen and sophomores, $4,000 a year for upperclassmen, and $7,500 a year for graduate students. Interest is currently 8%, rising to 10% after four years. Loans must be repaid within 10 years after graduation.

For those of you in lofty tax brackets, there is the **PLUS loan** (Parent Loan for Undergraduate Students). A spotless credit rating, not need, is the requirement here. Any parent can receive a PLUS loan of up to $4,000 a year from a bank, savings and loan, or credit union. The interest rate, which can be raised or lowered once a year, is set at 3.75 points above the one-year Treasury bill rate, not to exceed 12%. PLUS loans must be repaid within 10 years. The bad news: Payments begin 60 days after receiving the money.

State financial aid. Help is also available closer to home. More than $1 billion in aid is awarded by the fifty states each year to over one million undergraduates. Most state aid is offered only to residents attending in-state colleges. Check on this, however, because some states are more liberal.

Programs include grants, loans, work-study, discounts, and payment plans. Children planning to attend a private college in such states as Alabama, Florida, Georgia, Michigan, North Carolina, and Virginia can obtain tuition equalization grants to make up the difference between the average cost of private and public schools in the state.

State loans seldom require a showing of need. Terms and amounts vary from state to state. Generally, interest rates range between the federal rates for Stafford and PLUS loans, with repayment over 10 to 15 years.

Privately guaranteed loans. If you want to borrow a large sum at low interest, investigate such private, nonprofit underwriters as The Education Resources Institute (TERI) or Consern: Loans for Education. By guaranteeing payment, these agencies enable lenders to make educational loans without security. The agencies themselves are not lenders.

Through TERI, you may borrow from $2,000 to $20,000 per year at up to two points above the prime rate. There is also a 4% guarantee fee. You may begin repayment immediately or, if you prefer, pay interest only while your child remains in college. You may take up to 20 years to repay.

Consern generally limits borrowers to $15,000 at 4.1 points above its own index of commercial paper rates. It also charges a 4% guarantee fee, but gives you only 12 years to repay.

Please note that interest paid on educational loans from any source (other than those secured by your home equity) is not deductible.

Student employment. Colleges are expanding job opportunities, both on and off campus. **Work-study** programs offer jobs, at or near minimum wage, in the library, school cafeteria, or administrative offices. Earnings are paid directly to the student, not deducted from college costs, and are taxable.

Cooperative education programs let your child alternate a semester of study with a semester of work in his field of interest. Completing a degree usually takes five years, but your child's salary will offset the cost. Annual earnings are far above those paid work-study students and can cover all or most college costs. Your child does not have to qualify for financial aid to participate. For a free brochure, write to The National Commission for Cooperative Education, 360 Huntington Avenue, Boston, MA 02115.

If you can part with a little venture capital, your child can become an **undergraduate entrepreneur.** Who knows? The venture might even take off and become a career after graduation.

Service academies and ROTC. If you know a congressman and your child has a hankering for the wild blue yonder or the shores of Tripoli, try the military service academies. Not only will the government pay all expenses, it will throw in a monthly stipend. In return, your child makes a commitment to serve from four to eight years depending on the branch of service. But plan ahead—students must apply in their junior year.

ROTC scholarships pay tuition, fees, and books, plus a $100 monthly stipend. Students studying engineering, nursing, or the physical sciences have priority. Your child must agree to serve in the military after graduation for at least four years' active duty and two years' reserve duty. Again, plan on applying as early as March of the junior year.

Are you or your spouse veterans? If so, your child may be eligible for programs sponsored by the American Legion, the Veterans Administration, the individual branches of the military, and other organizations.

A listing of military-related programs can be found in *Need a Lift?,* published by the American Legion (National Emblem Sales, Box 1050, Indianapolis, IN 42606; $1 postpaid). Or see the *Directory of Financial Aid for Veterans, Military Personnel, and Their Dependents* by Schlacter and Weber, available in libraries.

Discounts and incentives. Cost-cutting gimmicks are proliferating as college expenses reach new highs. Among the bargains, discounts, and deals to explore:

- Discounts for academic excellence, such as graduating in the top 10% of the high school class
- Discounts for recruiting another student or other family members
- Discounts for children of alumni
- Discounts for attending evening or summer classes
- Differential pricing—for example, different tuition for different majors
- Anti-dropout discount or partial loan cancellation for graduating within four years
- Loan cancellation for academic achievement—for example, maintaining a 3.2 grade point average
- Grants for community or social service
- Loan forgiveness for future teachers, especially of math, science, and foreign languages

No matter how intimidating college costs appear, a college education is still possible for almost everyone. As we've seen, there are strategies you can use at every stage of childhood to build your college fund. Success, of course, depends on careful planning. Start early and make an ally of time. If time has deserted and left you to storm tuition costs alone, use the information in this chapter to uncover sources of financial aid. Help is available to the enterprising and the motivated.

10

YOU CAN'T
TAKE IT WITH YOU:
Estate Planning

Maybe you hope death will unreel like some Hollywood fantasy. You know. The one where you come back to earth as a guardian angel and straighten out the financial mess you left behind. If so, you're not alone. Every year, when I prepare my clients' tax returns, I hear the same refrain:

"We've been thinking. We probably should have a will."

I agree wholeheartedly.

"But not right away," they retreat. "After the filing season."

And then I sit, like the Maytag repairman, as the calendar leaves fall. No one calls.

A tombstone in Arizona reads, "Hung by mistake. The joke's on us." For the family and friends of those who die without an estate plan, it's all too true. The joke's on them. But the price the survivors must pay—in money and frustration—is no laughing matter.

The good news is that the protracted probate, unnecessary taxes, grasping lawyers, and rigid state laws that your heirs face can be avoided. Estate planning works. Not simply, to be sure. But with a well-drafted will and some deft legal maneuvering, you can spare your loved ones expense, worry, and reels of red tape. Wouldn't you rather be remembered with gratitude, than resentment?

You don't have to go it alone. In fact, you shouldn't. Yes, you can buy a book of forms or computer software and hammer out a do-it-yourself estate plan. But you do so at your heirs' peril. Estate planning is as complex as brain surgery, involving probate, trust, and tax laws that vary from state to state and a federal law that's changed more often than hotel linen. Only a skilled estate tax and trust attorney can design a plan that skirts the legal dangers, while meeting your specific needs.

But lawyers, like computers, are only as good as the information you feed them. The more you understand the basic tools of estate planning—wills, joint ownership, trusts, and lifetime giving—the better your chances of passing on your shared wealth without a hitch or disgruntled heirs.

Every estate plan has three goals: (1) easing the administrative burden of probate; (2) minimizing estate taxes; and (3) providing for heirs.

EASING THE BURDEN OF PROBATE

Property that passes under your will must go through probate. This is an archaic legal process in which your will is proved valid in a local court, your assets are inventoried, your debts, including death taxes, are paid, and the balance of your estate is distributed to your heirs.

If you die without a will, or your will isn't valid, your estate will also be subject to probate, through an "intestacy" proceeding. In effect, the court writes a will for you, distributing your property to your family as dictated by your state law. The court will also appoint a guardian for your minor children.

The aim of probate is to prevent fraud in transferring your property and to protect your heirs from never-ending creditors' claims. In reality, few heirs need these safeguards, and probate is largely a Kafkaesque form-filing marathon.

There are a host of reasons to avoid probate. Not the least is the cost. Although legal and administrative fees are limited by the states, they can still consume 5% to 10% of your estate.

Then there's the sheer inertia of the process. Enduring probate is like sitting in an airplane waiting for a turtle to cross the runway. Probate can take up to a year or more. Occasionally, a lot longer. I once represented a creditor of an estate that had been in probate for 10 years. My client's claim was settled in the twelfth year, but I still receive notices of new hearings—7 years later.

While probate grinds on, your heirs cannot touch your assets. This can create hardship for a family forced to meet living expenses on an income that has abruptly been halved. Furthermore, your estate may be wasting away due to inflation or a shifting economy. Few probate courts are concerned with managing your estate to protect its value.

Finally, probate is no respecter of privacy. The documents filed in a probate proceeding are matters of public record. Anyone can review the file. This is not to say a horde of your neighbors will descend on the courthouse, but if you want strict confidentiality, you should consider a trust (see below).

Not surprisingly, a number of legal methods have been devised to sidestep probate entirely. This is achieved by transferring your assets before death, instead of by will.

Deciding which of these methods, if any, is best for you is a major part of estate planning. Notice I said "if any." Probate is costly, true, but not any more than some of the trust arrangements engineered to avoid it. Probate is time-consuming, yes, but if your heirs will not be strapped for funds, the delay will be annoying, not fatal.

Moreover, disposing of your property, even on paper, makes investing clumsy and inconvenient. If you are a young couple, you may sensibly decide that wills are adequate for the time being to meet your twin needs of leaving property to the survivor and providing support and a guardian for your children if you die in a common accident. Probate avoidance can wait. It's unlikely that either of you will die soon, and your estates are still in the formative stages.

There are even several instances where probate is preferable. Because creditors of a probate estate must file claims within four to six months in order to be paid, probate is desirable if you die heavily in debt, perhaps as a result of a failing business. It is also advisable if you are a physician, dentist, lawyer, or other professional who might be subject to such claims as malpractice suits at a much later date. In that case, some small asset should be probated to cut off any future creditor's claims.

Also consider probate if you think your estate plan may be challenged in court.

Even if your estate will benefit from probate, a good estate plan should minimize the assets you transfer by will. Most probate courts have simplified, "express" procedures for closing small estates, and where fees are based on a percentage of the estate, costs can be cut significantly. The definition of a small estate varies from state to state, ranging from $500 in New Hampshire to $60,000 in California.

The principal methods of probate avoidance are bank account trusts, joint tenancy, living trusts, insurance, and gifts.

236 SPROUSE'S TWO-EARNER MONEY BOOK

Bank Account Trusts

There's a special type of bank account that skirts probate, lets you use and control your money during your life, and allows you to name the heir of your choice. Better still, it avoids the hazards of a joint bank account, where the other joint tenant can raid your funds before you die.

It's easy to set up. Open an account in your name as trustee for your beneficiary. While you're alive, the beneficiary has no right to any money in the account. But after your death, he or she can obtain ready access to the money by showing proof of identity and a certified copy of the death certificate.

This type of account goes by various names, including "informal trust," "Totten trust" (named after a court case establishing its validity), and "pay-on-death" accounts.

Whatever the name, you have the freedom to change beneficiaries, deposit or withdraw funds, and close the account at any time. Because you keep control, opening a bank account trust isn't subject to gift tax.

The weak points? Your money will be deposited in a bank savings account or certificate of deposit—a safe, but low-yielding investment. Note, however, that stocks, bonds, and other securities can also be designated as "payable on death" or "POD."

The money in this informal trust is also included in your taxable estate. Although it avoids probate, it does not escape federal estate tax if your estate exceeds $600,000 (the threshold for state death taxes varies).

Joint Tenancy

In some cases, holding property as joint tenants (or as tenants by the entirety) is an ideal way to avoid probate. Because title passes automatically to your surviving spouse when you die, jointly held assets bypass probate entirely.

The advantages of joint tenancy are discussed in Chapter 5. As an estate-planning tool, however, joint tenancy can create estate tax problems for couples with sizable estates.

How? An estate plan aims to apportion your assets so that the spouse who dies first won't saddle the survivor with a taxable estate of more than $600,000 (the amount exempt from federal tax). That way, the heirs won't be left with a hefty tax bill when the second spouse dies.

For example, Matt and Paula jointly own assets worth $750,000. If Matt were to die suddenly, his half of the joint property would pass to Paula tax-free, because married couples may leave estates of any size to each other without incurring tax. When Paula dies, however, her estate will exceed the $600,000 exemption amount by $150,000, and $54,700 will disappear into the black hole of the federal budget. If Matt and Paula held some of their property separately, each could have taken advantage of the $600,000 exemption.

Another shortcoming is that jointly held property can't be placed in trust for a spouse. Because irrevocable trusts are the escape routes from federal tax when your estate tops $600,000, holding property jointly prevents you from using this valuable estate-planning device. (See below for a discussion of irrevocable trusts.)

If you have already created joint tenancies, it's not too late to change them. But don't try to unravel them alone. Seek a lawyer.

Buy-sell agreements. If you are a joint owner of a closely held business or partnership, a buy-sell agreement can ensure that your heirs will dispose of your interest for a fair price. Under this type of agreement, the surviving shareholders or partners purchase your interest at a predetermined price.

This has the added advantage of fixing the value of your interest for estate tax purposes.

To guarantee that funds are available for the buyout, insure each shareholder's or partner's life, with the business named as the beneficiary and the proceeds earmarked for the purchase.

Living Trusts

Perhaps the most flexible and effective means of skipping probate is a living, or *inter vivos,* trust. Unlike a testamentary trust, which is created in your will and takes effect upon your death, a living trust swings into action while you are alive.

Living trusts may be revocable or irrevocable. Revocable trusts are more popular, because you continue to enjoy complete control over your property. You can spend the trust income, revise the trust's provisions, or terminate it. Most people even act as their own trustees.

While you're alive, therefore, a **revocable trust** is no more than a legal fiction. Although you put title to assets in the trust's name, it is merely your alter ego. Trust income is reported on your tax return if you or your spouse acts as trustee. And the assets placed in trust are included in your taxable estate. Revocable living trusts do not avoid death taxes.

At your death, however, the trust comes into its own. In effect, it does the work of a will, distributing its assets to your heirs or remaining in force for their benefit. Your wishes, as expressed in the trust instrument, are carried out by a successor trustee of your choice. None of the trust property passes through probate.

An **irrevocable living trust** operates exactly the same way upon your death. But when you establish an irrevocable trust, you no longer control the assets. Nor can you change the trust provisions. You give up all rights of ownership. For this reason, property in an irrevocable trust is not part of your taxable estate.

You can each set up living trusts for your separate property. If most or all of your assets are jointly owned, however, you should probably use one revocable living trust for your shared property. Otherwise ownership must be divided—a headache with assets such as real estate. And divvying up marital property can lead to unequal shares—for example, if his stock booms and hers goes bust.

Under a **shared or marital living trust,** each of you can name the beneficiaries of your portion of the trust property. When one of you dies, the marital property is divided, with the decedent's share going to his or her named beneficiaries—usually the surviving spouse or your children. Normally, if the surviving spouse inherits the property, he or she will transfer it to his or her living trust. *Note:* If your combined estate exceeds $600,000, you may need a more complex bypass living trust (see page 247).

A living trust has several secondary advantages. If you become incapacitated, the trust can spare you the cost and embarrassment of having a court appoint a conservator. Simply include a provision in the trust instrument allowing your successor trustee to take over if your doctor certifies that you are regrettably incompetent.

Unlike a will, a living trust can also protect your estate from creditors after your death. With a will, your executor must notify your creditors so they can submit claims against your estate. No such notice is required of a successor trustee. Creditors, however, can attach assets in a **revocable** living trust.

Lastly, the terms of your trust are private unless someone challenges its provisions. Such an attack is unlikely, though, because a living trust is harder to contest than a will.

Still, a living trust is no substitute for a will. For one thing, you can't use a trust to name a guardian for your minor children. For another, it's impossible to foresee and exempt every single asset from probate. What if your estate collects damages for your accidental death, for example? Again, you need a will—with a pour-over clause stating that any property you didn't put in your trust should be transferred there after your death.

Who should act as trustee? Most people appoint themselves as the initial trustee. If you set up a marital trust for jointly owned property, you and your spouse can serve as cotrustees. Name a successor trustee to take over when you die. If you have a modest-sized estate, it can probably be managed by your surviving spouse or a relative. Large estates may require professional management. Banks and trust companies provide this service for an average fee of 2% of the trust's assets. If you worry that an institutional trustee will not be responsive to your family's needs, appoint a family member or friend to act as cotrustee.

You must transfer your title in securities, real estate, or other assets to the living trust in order to avoid probate. Your trust will be worthless unless you do this. Attach a property schedule to the trust instrument. Keep this list up-to-date, revising it every time you add or withdraw assets. I have clients who have wasted $15,000 on estate plans that are worthless because they have neglected to transfer title to their living trusts.

Attorneys generally charge from $500 to $1,000 to draft revocable living trusts. The cost can exceed $10,000, however, depending upon the worth of your assets and the complexity of the trust provisions.

If you own real estate in more than one state, a living trust can spare your heirs the burden of multiple probates. For example, if you own property in three states, it may be necessary to open three probates (and enrich three lawyers). In some cases, a resident executor must also be appointed.

Assets with Named Beneficiaries

Certain assets are waved right through probate without stopping. Thus there is no need to transfer title in these assets to a living trust. These are any assets with named beneficiaries: corporate pension and profit-sharing plans, deferred compensation, annuities, savings bonds, Keogh and Individual Retirement Accounts, and life insurance policies.

MINIMIZING ESTATE AND INHERITANCE TAXES

This is a schizophrenic society. Our income tax law lets the rich get richer, while our estate tax law lops it off when they die. Politicians know it's not wise to back the rich into a corner, however. So the estate tax law is riddled with dozens of escape tunnels dug by fevered lawyers. With proper planning, there's no reason your children—and grandchildren—can't be born with platinum spoons in their mouths.

The federal estate tax is imposed on the value of your estate before it is distributed. Many states have estate or inheritance taxes as well (see page 254).

If you aren't on your guard, the tax bite can be vicious. The maximum estate tax is 55% on taxable estates of more than $3 million. For smaller estates, the plundering is less dramatic. But each tax dollar saved can be more critical to the heirs of a modest estate than it is to wealthier families.

Not every estate is taxed. You can dodge the federal estate tax bullet entirely by making sure the value of your taxable estate is less than $600,000. If your joint estate will clearly be worth less than $600,000, you can skip to the next section in this chapter.

Each of you may exempt $600,000. This means that you can leave a combined wealth of $1.2 million to your heirs tax-free. But not without some legal sleight-of-hand. So read on.

You may also make use of several other exemptions, including:

- all assets left to your surviving spouse (the marital deduction);
- gifts of up to $10,000 per person per year;
- all property left to a tax-exempt charity.

Before you can assess your tax peril, you must estimate the value of your taxable estate. The math is elementary. Add up your gross estate, then subtract allowable deductions and exemptions. Use the worksheet on page 263 to estimate your taxable estate.

Your Gross Estate

The first key to understanding the definition of gross estate is to realize that it has nothing to do with your will. Assets can be outside your will, but included in your gross estate—for example, property held in joint tenancy. (Joint-tenancy property automatically passes to the surviving joint tenant at your death, thereby bypassing your will. The value of your one-half interest in the property at your death is counted as part of your estate, however.)

Conversely, property distributable at your death can be outside your gross estate, for instance, insurance taken out by someone else on your life. If simply leaving property out of your will warded off taxes, there would be no need for tax planning. You could die intestate ("without a will," not "on a highway") and waltz through the pearly gates with a tax-free conscience.

In fact, your gross estate includes not only all property you own, but property over which you have control, even though you may not be legally entitled to a share of the property. This can happen if a relative gives you the power to dispose of his property after he dies, for example. You can even be taxed on property you once owned, but gave away. The federal estate and gift taxes are unified—the value of taxable gifts at the time you made them is added to the property you held at your death.

Among the taxable items commonly overlooked:

- **Annuities.** The value payable to the survivor is included to the extent of contributions made by you or your employer.
- **Jointly owned property.** One-half of the value of property held in joint tenancy with your spouse is included in the estate of the first spouse to die. The total value of property you own as a joint tenant with someone other than your spouse is included in the estate of the tenant who dies first, unless the survivor can prove he put up part of the purchase price or the property was received by gift or inheritance.
- **Insurance on your life.** Life insurance proceeds end up in your estate if you retain any rights of ownership. One solution: have your spouse own the policy on your life and vice versa. An even better answer may be an irrevocable life insurance trust (see page 250).
- **Insurance on another person's life.** If you insure each other as suggested, the cash surrender value of the

policy you hold on your spouse will be included in your gross estate.

- **Income payable after death.** If you die with your beeper on, any salary, commissions, or business income you earned before checking out will be paid to and included in your estate.
- **Pension and profit-sharing plan distributions.**
- **General power of appointment.** Only in the tax law could property you never owned be included in your estate if you are given a general power of appointment, that is, the right to say who that property will go to, including your estate or your creditors. This is true even if you didn't know you had the power. For example, Mildred wants her collection of antique musical instruments to go to any of her grandchildren with musical ability. Because they are all toddlers now, Mildred, in her will, grants her daughter Stacy a general power of appointment to give the instruments to whichever of her grandchildren prove to be budding Mozarts. If Stacy decides they all have tin ears, she can keep the instruments herself.
- **Retained life use or right to income.** Suppose you give your vacation home to your son, with the understanding that you can continue to use it whenever you like. The full value will be included in your estate. The same if you transfer all of your assets to a living trust, reserving the right to any income the trust earns.
- **A reversionary interest.** If your gift comes back to you after a specified number of years or if you outlive the donee, you are the owner for estate tax purposes. Even the remotest chance that the property will revert causes its inclusion in your estate. Suppose, for example, that you set up a trust with the income payable to your son for life, with the remainder to your granddaughter—

unless you're still alive. Who's the effective owner? You are. The odds may be a million to one, but you could outlive your granddaughter. More power to you.

Deductions

Now that you have a rough idea of your gross estate, the next step is to determine your deductions. Your executor may subtract:

- Expenses of your last illness
- Funeral expenses
- Probate fees and expenses, such as legal and accounting fees and executors' commissions
- Mortgages and other unpaid bills
- Bequests or gifts to charity (for a discussion of charitable trusts, see page 252)

If you are the first spouse to die, your estate also benefits from the most valuable write-off of all: the marital deduction.

Marital Deduction

All property left to your surviving spouse is exempt from federal estate tax. This marital deduction postpones taxation of your two estates until both of you pass on. Thus, your family receives the income from the assets that would have gone to pay taxes when its need is greatest.

Generally, assets are willed to the surviving spouse outright. She or he has unconditional use of the property. In some cases, however, a spouse may want to leave property in trust. Only two types of trusts qualify for the marital deduction.

Marital deduction trusts. With a **general power of appointment trust,** you put your assets in trust for your spouse, but appoint an adult child, say, as trustee. Your spouse is the sole beneficiary with a general power of appointment, that is, your spouse decides who ultimately inherits the property. This somewhat obsolete form of trust is used most often when a spouse is incapacitated or otherwise unable to manage property.

If you want the final say over who receives your assets, consider a **qualified terminal interest (QTIP) trust.** Under this trust, your spouse must receive all of the trust income for life. The principal goes to your choice of heirs after your surviving spouse dies. QTIPs are commonly used to prevent a spouse from cutting off children from a prior marriage.

The second death. This isn't the title of a mystery novel; it's a dilemma. You see, the marital deduction merely delays the day of tax reckoning. The bill comes due when your surviving spouse dies—if inheriting your property has increased her or his estate to over $600,000.

Let's take Alan and Connie, for example. They estimate that their aggressive financial planning will boost their marital estate to $1,500,000 in their golden years. Each of them is entitled to a $600,000 estate tax exclusion. With proper planning, they can leave $1,200,000 to their children with no federal estate taxes.

Suppose Alan dies first. No federal estate taxes will be due, because all property left to a surviving spouse is exempt from estate tax. It doesn't matter how much property Alan leaves—$10 or $10,000,000. None of it is included in his taxable estate. In effect, Alan's $600,000 exemption is lost— because it isn't needed.

When Connie passes away, however, all of her estate in excess of $600,000 will be taxed. The loss of Alan's exemption will cost the estate (and their children) an additional $156,500 in estate tax.

To prevent this calamity from happening to you, more creative and complex measures are called for.

Trimming Your Estate

The only way to cut your estate down to nontaxable size is by pitching assets overboard. This is accomplished chiefly by trusts and gifts.

Bypass trust. With large estates, the marital deduction may not completely wipe out taxes. The surviving spouse needs the full benefit of his or her $600,000 exemption, too. But with a bypass trust you can leave up to $1.2 million to your ultimate heirs tax-free. The trust is designed to give the surviving spouse the benefit of the trust's income during his or her lifetime. Actual title to the property "bypasses" the surviving spouse, however. At the surviving spouse's death, the trust assets are distributed tax-free to the beneficiaries (usually the children).

Here's how it works: Suppose Hal and Anne have assets of $1.2 million, $800,000 of which is in his name and $400,000 is in hers. If Hal leaves Anne all of his property, he condemns her $1.2 million estate to paying $235,000 in taxes. Instead, he can bequeath up to $600,000 tax-free in his will to a bypass trust. The $200,000 balance of his estate goes directly to Anne, and thanks to the marital deduction, it also eludes tax.

Anne can collect the trust's income for life, plus up to $5,000 or 5% a year of the principal, whichever is greater. When Anne dies, the trust ends, and the remaining assets go to the heirs Hal named in his will. Because Anne's estate won't exceed $600,000, it, too, will be exempt from tax.

What happens to this best-laid plan if Hal and Anne die simultaneously? Because his estate is the larger, Hal should provide in his will that Anne be presumed the survivor if they die in each other's arms.

Trusts are gratifying in the way of all intricate legal schemes: they make us feel like we're getting our money's worth. There is a simpler way to reduce "second death" taxes, though. You and your spouse can leave up to $600,000 of your separate property directly to your children.

Irrevocable living trust. You can whisk an asset out of your estate without making an outright gift by transferring title to an irrevocable living trust. The catch? You give up all rights to the trust income and principal during your life. You are free to name the income beneficiary and to designate who will inherit the principal. But you can't change your mind later about who gets what and when.

Because transfers to an irrevocable living trust are considered gifts, you may owe gift tax if you put in more than $10,000 per year.

Life insurance. In *Take the Money and Run,* Woody Allen, as a convicted robber, tries to make his escape. He's caught and given the worst punishment our penal system can devise—a month in solitary with an insurance salesman. Despite this unenviable image, life insurance is a relatively inexpensive and flexible way to solve several estate problems, including:

- **Income replacement.** Life insurance assures that the loss of your income won't lower your family's standard of living and that little Dana can go on to college.
- **Liquidity.** The high cost of dying can strain even the biggest estate if its assets cannot be readily converted

to cash. Your estate could suffer a substantial loss if your heirs were forced to sell hastily such illiquid assets as real estate or a small business interest in order to meet pressing bills. Insurance proceeds provide cash to pay death taxes, as well as debts and funeral expenses.

- **Probate avoidance.** Generally, insurance proceeds escape probate because the beneficiary is named in the policy, not in your will.

Just because it's desirable to *have* life insurance (and you should evaluate your needs) doesn't necessarily mean you should *own* it. Why? Because any policy you own and on which you paid the premiums are included in your taxable estate. Even though your spouse and children are the named beneficiaries, the IRS can cut itself in for a share of the proceeds. Say, for example, your estate (without the marital deduction) is unlucky enough to be in the 39% bracket and the policy is for $200,000. The tax man would snatch $78,000 before your heirs got within spitting distance.

Any incident of ownership will corral your life insurance into your taxable estate. You don't have to be the registered owner. It's enough if you have the right to name or change beneficiaries; borrow against the policy or pledge the policy; surrender, convert, or cancel it; select a payment option; or pay the premiums.

One solution, as we have seen, is for spouses to cross-insure each other. You take out a policy and pay the premiums on your spouse's life, and he or she does the same on yours. If you already own a policy on your life, you can transfer it to your spouse or adult child and have him or her pay the premiums. *Note:* Such a transfer is treated as a gift and may be subject to gift tax if the cash value of the policy exceeds $10,000.

Before giving up ownership, consider whether you want to take such an irreversible step. Are you sure you will never need to borrow the cash value? Or change the beneficiary? What if your marriage ends in divorce? Will you want your ex-spouse to collect?

Then, too, transferring ownership to your spouse doesn't solve the problem of the second death. If your life insurance policies are sizable enough to push the surviving spouse's estate over the $600,000 mark, you need a better answer. It comes—no surprise—in the form of a trust.

Irrevocable life insurance trust. You can remove life insurance policies—even employer-paid group term policies—from your taxable estate by handing them over to an irrevocable trust. You must give up all ownership rights and cannot act as trustee. The cash value, if any, of the policy at the time it is transferred, along with any subsequent premium payments, are regarded as gifts. To the extent they exceed $10,000, they are added to your taxable estate.

At your death, the insurance proceeds go into the trust untaxed, and in most cases, your spouse receives the income that the trust earns for the rest of her or his life, plus any principal needed to cover living expenses. When your spouse dies, the trust ends and the remaining assets pass to the beneficiaries named in your will.

Don't attempt to set up an irrevocable life insurance trust without the help of a witch doctor or a lawyer.

Three-year rule. In football, a quarterback can't toss the ball to his receivers if he finds himself "in the grasp." The IRS has a similar rule. You can't pass insurance policies to your spouse or children if you suddenly learn Death has thrown a block at your ankles. If you die within three years of giving away a policy, including placing it in trust, the penalty is inclusion in your taxable estate.

The only way around this rule is to cash in your current policies and have the trustee take out new insurance on your life. If you don't cotton to this plan, have your attorney insert a clause in the trust instrument stating that the proceeds should go directly to your spouse or a marital deduction trust if you die within three years.

GRITs. If your combined estates will exceed $1.2 million, consider a **grantor retained income trust (GRIT)**—especially if you own rapidly appreciating property.

With a GRIT, you put property in an irrevocable trust, reserving the right to receive all the trust income for up to 10 years. Neither you nor your spouse can serve as trustee. When the trust terminates at the end of the specified number of years, the property goes to your chosen beneficiaries.

What makes a GRIT so appealing is that you are assumed to have transferred only the actuarial value of the property that ultimately passes to your heirs. This remainder interest amounts to a fraction of what you actually place in trust.

Suppose Hannah places stock worth $1 million in a GRIT that will end in 10 years. The value of Hannah's income interest and her daughter's remainder interest are computed by the IRS using special tables. The value of the income interest is currently $600,152, and the trust's remainder interest is $399,848. Because the remainder interest weighs in at far less than the $600,000 exemption, there is no estate tax. Assuming the stocks appreciate at the rate of 7% a year, Hannah's daughter will inherit $1,967,151 tax-free.

There is one danger. If Hannah dies before the trust ends, the stocks will be included in her estate. Her daughter can protect herself by insuring Hannah's life to pay the estate tax.

Trust Variations

You can also keep your estate out of tax's way by giving assets to charity. With a **charitable remainder trust,** you or members of your family collect all the trust income for a specified time, usually until the death of your surviving spouse. The trust then terminates, and the charity receives outright ownership of the assets.

The trust can be created by will or while you're alive. In the former case, the donated property is included in your taxable estate, but a portion of its value is deductible. If you set up a living trust, you may generally claim a charitable contribution in the year that the trust begins.

You can increase your estate's tax deduction with a testamentary **charitable lead trust.** This is the reverse of a charitable remainder trust. The charity receives the income until the trust ends at your death, when your beneficiaries inherit the assets.

If you have grandchildren, a **generation-skipping trust** may be attractive. The trust income generally goes to one of your children. After your child dies, the trust dissolves, and any remaining assets go to one or more of your grandchildren. The assets of the trust are included in your estate. The big tax saving comes when your child dies. Generation-skipping trust assets of up to $1 million ($2 million for married couples) are exempt from estate tax.

Gifts

By far the simplest way to jettison assets is to give them away. You may give as much as $10,000 a year to any number of lucky donees without touching off the gift tax. Married couples can make joint gifts of up to $20,000 tax-free.

In addition to the $10,000 exclusion, the following gifts are tax-exempt: (1) gifts to your spouse, (2) payments to health-care and educational institutions to cover a friend's or relative's medical or tuition expenses, and (3) gifts to charity.

Although gifts of any size to your spouse are tax-free, you may be wiser to rely on the marital deduction. Why? Because a gift can result in substantial—and unnecessary—capital gains. That's because when you make a gift to your spouse, you are also giving her or him your basis in the property. For example, if you give your spouse land that you bought in Alaska for $15,000, your spouse's basis in the land will also be $15,000. If your spouse sells the land for $25,000 when you die, she or he will owe tax on a $10,000 taxable gain. On the other hand, if the land passes to your spouse in your will, its basis will be the fair market value at your death, or $25,000. So when your spouse sells the property for $25,000, he or she will have no taxable gain at all.

Another benefit of relying on the marital deduction instead of making a gift is that the property won't return to you automatically if your spouse dies first. And if you divorce, your spouse would, I feel sure, keep the gift.

Don't let the tax benefits of gift giving outweigh other financial concerns. Remember that a gift cannot be undone. Large gifts can jeopardize your security if you suffer a business reversal or personal misfortune. And your surviving spouse will have no access to money you give away, which isn't necessarily the case with trusts. It's prudent, therefore, to make gifts only if you're certain your estate will be taxable and both of you will have enough income to live on.

You will realize the greatest tax savings if you give away property with growth potential. Give high-tech stock worth

$10,000 today, and you may remove $100,000 from your estate when the shares shoot up tomorrow.

Reporting to the IRS. A gift of $10,000 or less is not news. You do not have to report it to the IRS. If your spouse consents to make a joint gift of more than $10,000, a return must be filed even though the total was within the allowable $20,000 exclusion. File Form 709A by April 15 of the year following the year of the gift. If you request an extension for filing your income tax return, you may get the same extension for filing the gift tax return.

If you exceed the annual exclusion amount, you don't have to pay the IRS right away. Instead, the taxable gifts you make during your lifetime are subtracted from your $600,000 estate tax exemption. If you give $50,000 individually to your sister this year and meet your Maker the next, you would have only a $550,000 estate tax exclusion.

State Death Taxes

The federal government is not the only scavenger hovering over your grave—the states are gleefully poised there, too. With the exception of Nevada, all the states impose death taxes.

These taxes are trivial in comparison with the federal estate tax, however. And twenty-four states plus the District of Columbia collect only a "pick-up" tax equal to the maximum credit for state taxes allowed on the federal estate tax return. Part of the federal estate tax is paid to the state instead. So your estate pays no more total tax than if the state imposed no death taxes.

The remaining states impose death taxes on (1) all residents' personal property and (2) all real estate owned in the state, no matter where you call home. Some states also levy an inheritance tax on your heirs.

The same tactics for avoiding federal estate taxes apply to state death taxes. But be wary in the nine states that impose gift taxes (Delaware, Louisiana, New York, North Carolina, Oregon, Rhode Island, South Carolina, Tennessee, and Wisconsin). You may not be able to give away as much tax-free in these states as federal law allows.

PROVIDING FOR HEIRS

There's only one excuse for not having a will: you're flat broke, alone, and living out of a shopping cart. Even then, you may want to make sure your grate-mate gets your rags.

Dying intestate—without a valid will—is impossibly careless, like striking a match to find a gas leak or losing your child. But don't worry. Your state will step in and hack up your estate like a watermelon, freely giving slices away to your hands-stretched-out relatives. Some of them may even be deserving.

Of course, your spouse will get a share—to the extent that state law allows. Depending on where you live, your spouse will be entitled to from one-third to one-half of your estate. In some states, the surviving spouse's share is equal to a child's share. If you have four children, your spouse will get only one-fifth. The rest will be divided evenly among your children, regardless of their ages or special needs. Your devil-may-care attitude can strand your spouse with a subsistence income in old age, put money into the hands of children too immature to handle it, and leave your alma mater and old Spot out in the cold.

"But we own everything jointly," you say. "If I die my

spouse gets my half of everything. No fuss, no probate, no will." No problem? Not if you are childless and both of you die in a car crash. If you die instantly and your spouse lingers on for a day or two, your half of the joint property would automatically pass to your spouse on your death. Bad news for *your* relatives. All of your assets will go to your spouse's heirs.

And what if you have children? Sure, your jointly owned property would pass to them under state intestacy laws if you perish together. But how would responsibility for caring for your children and their inheritances pass? If you die without a will, the court must appoint a guardian. Normally the court will appoint a relative, but it could as easily be your boorish, loudmouthed brother-in-law as kindly, comforting Aunt Mary.

You get the point. Even if your estate plan has all the bells, whistles, and trusts necessary to avoid probate and to render the estate tax powerless, you need at least a simple will for the following reasons:

- **To name a personal guardian to care for your minor children.** This can't be done using a trust. You can appoint a property guardian as well, although it's usually better to use your will to create a trust for your children's property.
- **To name your executor.** You want your estate managed honestly and efficiently. If you die without a will and able relatives, the court may tap a political crony or even a creditor to act as administrator. This official generally receives fees of 3% to 5% of your estate. Administrators must also post a bond, the premium coming out of your estate. If you have a living trust, name your successor trustee to serve as executor.

- **To distribute property not transferred by a probate avoidance device.** A will can be a valuable backup if you acquired property that you had no time to, or neglected to, transfer out of your estate.

Don't practice false economy by drafting your own will. If your estate is simple—less than $600,000 with no out-of-state real estate—hiring a lawyer will set you back a mere $75 to $200. The bargain lure of how-to books and do-it-yourself forms can lead to disaster. Your homemade will can founder on a technicality. Remember, an invalid will is no different from no will at all.

By all means brag about your new wills at wine tastings, but don't forget about them when your friends become bored. Things change. You should review your wills every three years and amend them if (1) a child or grandchild is born (unless your will provides for children born after it was signed); (2) you divorce or separate; (3) a beneficiary dies; (4) federal or state tax laws change; (5) you move to another state; (6) you become substantially richer or poorer; or (7) you have a change of heart about how to divide your property.

Minor changes can be made by asking your lawyer to add a codicil to your will. Whatever you do, don't scribble on your will yourself. You may unwittingly invalidate it and send your careful planning up in smoke.

Marriage and Your Will

Before you declare you're of sound mind and body, the two of you should have a frank discussion to resolve any conflicts. This is especially true if either or both of you have ex-spouses and children from prior marriages. I have seen jealousies among stepfamilies that would make Cinderella feel loved. One common point of contention is who should care for the children. Quite naturally, each spouse usually favors his or her own side of the family. There are no pat answers. Each couple has to reach its own compromise.

Your spouse's minimum share. State laws protect a spouse from being disinherited or receiving too little after the other spouse's death. In community-property states, legal safeguards aren't needed because each spouse owns one-half of all property acquired during marriage out of the couple's joint earnings. Separate property can be left to whomever a spouse pleases.

In most separate-property states, a spouse is entitled to one-third of the other's property. The statutory share is one-half in a few states. The exact share can depend on how many children you have.

In some states, only a percentage of the property transferred by will must go to the survivor. In others, property that passes both through and outside probate is counted.

What happens if you accidentally or deliberately leave your spouse less than the law allows? Generally, your spouse has a choice: to take under the will or to take the minimum share permitted by law ("take against the will"). If a spouse decides to claim his or her statutory share, your other heirs are obviously going to get far less than you intended.

If you are bent on disinheriting your spouse, the most effective way is to get him or her to sign a prenuptial agreement.

Moving from state to state. Crossing state lines does not invalidate a will or living trust. The ownership of your property can change, however, if you move from a separate-property state to a community-property state or vice versa.

Suppose you acquire stocks in Iowa, a separate-property state. If you move to the community-property states of California or Idaho, the stocks will be treated according to community-property rules under the laws of those two states. But if you leave Iowa for one of the other community-property states (Arizona, Nevada, New Mexico, Texas, Washington, or Wisconsin), the stocks will keep their original character as separate property.

When spouses change directions and move from community-property to separate-property states, each generally keeps his or her one-half interest in the community property.

Simultaneous death. When you go, do you want to go together? Then you'd better add appropriate provisions to your wills. Because if property is left to your spouse without a clause covering simultaneous death, and that's what happens, your property could pass to your spouse and then immediately to your spouse's heirs. While your own heirs go begging.

To prevent this, your wills should contain "simultaneous death" clauses, providing that if you die at the same time, you are both presumed to have outlived the other. Thus, your property goes to the person next in line to your spouse on your beneficiary list. Your spouse's property does the same.

For example, Meg and Dennis leave everything to each other in their wills. But Meg wants her property to go to her sister Diana if Dennis dies before she does. Dennis wants his son Todd to have his property if Meg predeceases him. As bad luck would have it, Meg and Dennis die tangled in each other's parachutes in a freak skydiving accident. Under their simultaneous death clauses, Meg's property will go to her sister and Dennis's to his son.

Joint wills. A joint will is *one* document signed by two spouses and serving as both their wills. Each spouse leaves everything to the other when the first one dies. The will then specifies how the property will be distributed at the second death. In theory, a joint will guarantees that the surviving spouse can't dispose of the money in a way that would cause the first decedent to turn over in his or her grave. A legal handcuff, if you will, tying the hands of the survivor.

A joint will is not recommended. They can confound probate, tie up property for years until the survivor dies, and provoke endless legal wrangles about whether or not any part of the will can be revoked or changed. If you want control over property that you leave to your spouse, look into a marital deduction trust instead (see page 246).

Children and Wills

Providing for your minor children if you die raises two concerns: (1) who will raise the children and (2) how will they be supported?

Custody. Where there are two willing and capable parents, and one dies, the survivor generally has the legal right to assume sole custody. But what if you both die? Then some other adult must become the child's personal guardian.

Your child's personal guardian must be named in your will, and your choice must be approved by a court. Normally, a judge will reject a nominee only if someone contests his competence or the court has evidence of severe problems, such as alcoholism or mental instability.

Once you and your spouse have decided on a guardian, secure an agreement in advance. You can ask, but not force, a friend or relative to take custody. One possibility, if that person has a young child, too, is to enter into a reciprocal agreement under which the surviving couple will raise the other's children.

Name an alternate guardian as well, in case your first choice is unavailable or at the last minute unwilling to serve.

If you believe a former spouse or relative will dispute the guardian you name, consult a family lawyer.

Providing Financial Support

Minor children cannot own more than a minimal amount of property outright. You must, therefore, name a guardian for your child's property, too. This includes the property you leave for his benefit as well as his earnings or any other assets acquired by inheritance or gift.

Whom should you choose? Someone with integrity and common sense. Financial wizardry is not required. The same person you choose to take custody is most sensible, unless he or she is completely inexperienced in managing property. Similarly, your alternate personal guardian can be named stand-in property guardian.

Banks and trust companies make poor property guardians. If the property is worth less than $200,000, they simply won't bother. Then, too, they nick accounts for every phone call and paper clip. And even though your child won't have to beg like Oliver Twist for more, banks are too impersonal to respond adequately to a child's needs.

How to leave property. Support for your child can be provided in two ways. You can leave property to your child under your will, to be supervised by the property guardian you name. But this method is cumbersome and inefficient because the guardian, even if he or she is the parent, must often get permission from the court to pay the child's expenses from the legacy and must account for the assets' management. A boon for your lawyer, but not for your heirs. Furthermore, the guardian must spend the money that you leave as state law dictates.

Far better is to create a trust to hold your child's inheritance. The trustee you select will generally be free of court supervision and reporting requirements. Instead, the trustee will follow your instructions as set forth in the trust instrument. With a trust, you specify the age at which your child comes into his inheritance. A guardian must surrender control of property when your child is 18.

Your child's trust can be testamentary, that is, established by your will. Or you can avoid probate by creating a living trust for each child. Trustees are usually given the power to spend any of the trust income or principal for your child's health, education, or living expenses. When your child reaches the designated age, the trust ends and the remaining trust property is distributed to him.

Even if you rely on a trust to finance your child's upbringing, you should still name a property guardian in your will to supervise any property not included in the trust, such as a large gift your child receives after you die.

If the value of the property you leave your child is less than $25,000, a trust will not be economical. A more practical option would be to leave the property directly to your spouse (or the child's parent) or to your child under the Uniform Gifts to Minors Act (see Chapter 8).

ESTIMATED ESTATE TAX WORKSHEET

1. Gross estate $ _____
2. Less: Deductions
   a. Outstanding debts $ _____
   b. Funeral/last illness   _____
   c. Taxes due   _____
   d. Administrative
      costs   _____
                                             (_____)

3. Subtotal of deductions
   (lines 2a, b, c, d)   (_____)

4. Adjusted gross estate
   (line 1 minus line 3)   _____
5. Less: Marital
           deduction   (_____)

6. Less: Charitable
           contributions   (_____)

7. Plus: Taxable gifts made
           after 1976   _____
8. Taxable estate
   (line 4 plus line 7
   minus lines 5 and 6)   _____
9. Federal estate tax before
   credits (find the amount
   on line 8 in column A of
   the table below and read
   across to column B)   _____
10. Less: Federal unified
         credit   (192,800   )

11. Net federal estate tax   _____
12. Less: Maximum credit for
            state death taxes
            (column C below)   (_____)

13. Estated federal estate tax
    (line 11 minus line 12) $ _____

A Taxable Estate	B Federal Estate Tax Before Credits	C Maximum Credit For State Death Taxes
$ 50,000	$ 10,600	$ 0
100,000	23,800	0
200,000	54,800	1,200
300,000	87,800	3,600
400,000	121,800	6,800
500,000	155,800	10,000
600,000	192,800	14,000
700,000	229,800	18,000
800,000	267,800	22,800
900,000	306,800	27,600
1,000,000	345,800	33,200
1,200,000	427,800	45,200
1,500,000	555,800	64,400
2,000,000	780,800	99,600
$3,000,000	$1,290,000	$182,000

ESTATE PLANNING TIPS

FOR ANY SIZE ESTATE

• Inventory your assets
  —Project future accumulation of wealth and estimate size of your estate.
  —If combined estate will exceed $600,000, estate tax planning is needed (see tips in "For Combined Estates over $600,000" below).

• Evaluate your family's financial needs in the event of death, and purchase life insurance to maintain family's standard of living and to cover projected estate tax.

• Designate beneficiaries for your IRAs, Keoghs, pension and profit-sharing plans, and life insurance policies.

- Make sure you fully understand your pension plan and employee benefits.

- To avoid probate, consider:
  —Putting assets in joint tenancy with your spouse (if combined estate will be less than $600,000).
  —Setting up a living trust
    —Use one trust for shared property; separate trusts for separate property.
    —Draft pour-over will to transfer assets you failed to put in trust before your death.
    —Transfer title of assets to living trust.
    —If your combined estate exceeds $600,000, you may need a bypass living trust (see p. 247).

- Draft a will
  —Leave assets valued at less than $600,000 to designated heirs.
  —Make specific bequests of personal items, e.g., jewelry.
  —Choose contingent beneficiaries in case your first choices die before you do.
  —Name a personal guardian for minor children.
  —Set up a testamentary trust for minor or disabled children.
  —Appoint a property guardian for trust property.
  —Add a "simultaneous death" clause.
  —Name an executor to administer your estate.
  —Store your will somewhere safe from fire or other damage. A safe deposit box can be used if your state's law permits survivors to retrieve wills from boxes immediately after death. In some states, you may deposit your will with the probate court. Other alternatives: leave your will with your lawyer or buy a fireproof file cabinet or home safe.
  —Review your will every 3 years; update as necessary.

- Inform your spouse and adult family members where your will is kept, who has been named executor, and where to find life insurance policies.

- Record location of your bank accounts, stocks, bonds, real estate, and important papers.

• Inform family about plans made, or requests you have, for your funeral, including location of deed for burial plot, prepaid funeral arrangements, and organ donations.

• Make a list of persons to be notified of your death.

• Draw up a set of procedures for survivors to follow to ensure that everything goes smoothly after death.

• Plan the succession or disposal of your self-employed business.

• Plan for incapacity
—Purchase adequate disability insurance.
—Grant a durable power of attorney to your spouse, enabling him or her to make medical and financial decisions if you become mentally or physically unable to do so.

FOR COMBINED ESTATES OVER $600,000

• Begin a program of lifetime giving to friends and relatives (up to $10,000 per donee a year tax-free—up to $20,000 jointly).

• Make tax-free gifts to charities.

• Put life insurance into an irrevocable life insurance trust (see p. 250).

• Choose a sophisticated executor for your estate—investigate institutional trust departments to determine fees.

• Use a bypass trust for the portion of your estate equal to the $600,000 federal exclusion for estate and gift tax (see p. 247).
—Bequeath the rest of your estate to your spouse, either outright or in trust to take advantage of the marital deduction.

• Consider the use of the following trusts:
—General power of appointment trust (see p. 246).
—Qualified terminal interest (QTIP) trust (see p. 246).
—Irrevocable living trust (see p. 248).
—Grantor retained income trust (see p. 251).
—Charitable remainder or charitable lead trust (see p. 252).

AFTERWORD

Doonesbury cartoonist Garry Trudeau summed up his philosophy at an awards dinner in Los Angeles. "I'm trying to develop a life-style that doesn't require my presence," he said. I imagine a lot of us feel the same way about our finances. We're hoping to find a system of wealth-building that doesn't require our management.

I'd like to be encouraging. But to paraphrase the comic whose story falls flat, "You really have to be there." Sure, you can hire blue-ribbon professionals—it's a sensible solution for two-earners on the go. But the ultimate responsibility is yours. Unless you play an active role, the power of your two paychecks will never be realized.

You now have the knowledge to take those first, halting investment steps. Once you get started, you'll be amazed at how the pace picks up. Money is magnetic. It attracts more wealth.

So what are you waiting for? Some parting words of advice? All right. Build an emergency fund. Save, save, save. Cut down on consumer debt. Diversify. Don't use "busy" as an excuse for not setting and making financial goals. For heaven's sake, write wills. Acquire real estate with the zeal of a *Monopoly* champion. Manage your child's finances as astutely as your own. Hang up when a stranger offers you riches on the phone. Never believe an ad claiming you can gross $1,000,000 in just three months.

Anything else?

Just the obligatory pep talk. There's no time like the present. You can do anything if you put your minds to it. Dress warmly. Don't forget to share the derring-do, as well as the drudgery. And, oh yes, enjoy yourselves.

INDEX